The Brazen Plagiarist

The Brazen Plagiarist:
Selected Poems

KIKI DIMOULA

TRANSLATED BY

CECILE INGLESSIS MARGELLOS

AND RIKA LESSER

YALE UNIVERSITY PRESS ■ NEW HAVEN & LONDON

A MARGELLOS
WORLD REPUBLIC OF LETTERS BOOK

The Margellos World Republic of Letters is dedicated to making literary works from around the globe available in English through translation. It brings to the English-speaking world the work of leading poets, novelists, essayists, philosophers, and playwrights from Europe, Latin America, Africa, Asia, and the Middle East to stimulate international discourse and creative exchange.

Yale University Press books may be purchased in quantity for educational, business, or promotional use. For information, please e-mail sales.press@yale.edu (U.S. office) or sales@yaleup.co.uk (U.K. office).

Set in Electra type by Tseng Information Systems, Inc. Printed in the United States of America.

Library of Congress Cataloging-in-Publication Data
Demoula, Kike.
[Poems. English. Selections]
The brazen plagiarist : selected poems / Kiki Dimoula ; translated by Cecile Inglessis Margellos and Rika Lesser. — 1st ed.
p. cm. — (Margellos World Republic of Letters)
"A Margellos World Republic of Letters book."
Includes bibliographical references.
ISBN 978-0-300-14139-9 (alk. paper)
I. Margellos, Cecile Inglessis, 1953– II. Lesser, Rika. III. Title.
PA5615.E474A2 2012
889'.134—dc23

2012019119

A catalogue record for this book is available from the British Library.

This paper meets the requirements of ANSI/NISO Z39.48–1992 (Permanence of Paper).

10 9 8 7 6 5 4 3 2 1

For my husband, Theodore, who makes all impossible things possible
   C.I.M.

In memory of Etta Veit-Simon Japha,
whose life spirit, families, and countries also are mine
   R.L.

CONTENTS

THOUGHTS OF AN AWKWARD IMMIGRANT
TO A FOREIGN LANGUAGE

Kiki Dimoula

And yet I'm traveling. I'm going to the magnificent English language, unknown to me, though sixty years ago I lived in London for several months and learned to mumble the alphabet of elementary communication—those few phrases necessary to sustain the illusion that we know what we don't.

Years later, I had to return to England more than once, but for far less joyful reasons. Still this dismal difference never reclaimed the sparkling gift of the unprecedented bestowed by my first visit. Yes, in London my sense of fleeing—untouched and chaste until then—lost its virginity.

My ecstatic strolling through the parks, whose welcoming moist grass promised velvet continuity to my steps, is still green in my memory. Green, too, remains the mysterious gray of London's atmosphere, where my soul was probably initiated into a similar grayness.

But the important thing is that I'm going to an unknown language filled with apprehension, even if they say that, knowing how the universal is spoken, poetry is in no danger of losing its way in any worldly unknown.

Anyway, the few things I've written in my life set out on this journey accompanied by an excellent letter of introduction—their translation. This time it is signed by two heroic translators, Cecile Inglessis Margellos and Rika Lesser. I say heroic because I believe that translation is an act of self-abandonment, indeed of self-oblivion, so the translator may enter unprejudiced into otherness; so she may break through the secretive precautions the impulsive wording takes in order to prevent its immediate consumption by perception's voracious ease.

The only painless duty of the translator is bringing the dictionaries of two languages, strangers to one another, face to face and forcing them to speak to each other. But her heaviest and most exhausting task, henceforth tantamount to an ex nihilo creation, is convincing a word to leave its country and entrust its meaning—great or small—to an unknown guardianship.

Not easy at all. Each word has its life, its past, its ego, its self-esteem. It resists. It doesn't want to leave all this to the mercy of some foreign handling, however reverential. If you promise a poem that, translated, it will be rid of its imperfections, that its dissonance will become harmonious, that its level of transcendence, dreamed but not attained, will heighten, I suspect it will not consent—at least not willingly. An honest poem will not easily disavow even its most humble origin.

I know well by instinct how much a word will torment the translator before conceding to its emigration. And maybe I would interpret this resistance as the word's vindictiveness against its identity's abductor.

More simply, every word driven from its homeland by translation is afraid that in the other land, the other language, the ashes of its feelings may get scattered, that no appropriate urn for words will be found there for the safekeeping of purposelessness—who knows what other countries' traditions about decay can be? Every native word fears that translation may not hermetically seal memory's little phial, and that the past, fleeting in any case, will instantly evaporate.

The translatable has these and other worries—for instance, whether the bridge from one language to another is sound enough, whether it can bear the weight of a word's rhythm, since its rhythm does not stand alone but is inseparable from that of its neighbors.

Will translation's bridge support the heavy load of interpretative clothing meaning brings with it? Meaning fears it will be allowed only one piece, the most superficial and, hence, very conveniently, the lightest possible for a safe crossing to the comprehensible.

Fortunately, what I have written is not anxious, not crabby, not arrogant; it does not believe in the untranslatability of its very light aspiration, which is none other than to find a place to hide myself, so that I or my writings will not be discovered too soon by decay. Besides, isn't art's secret aim to erect a statue in honor of the temporary, charitably delayed?

I rest assured that the translators of my small wings will not force them to fly too high and that they will keep hushed the scream of this old line of mine: "Bending down, I was gazing at the sky," a line supportive of every discouragement.

I am grateful to both translators for their redeeming solutions to the problems of my written life. I thank Rika, whom I know only through Cecile's introductory praise and her subsequent reassertions of her co-translator's linguistic craftsmanship and infallible translational ethics. But most of all I thank Cecile, who inspired my admiring comments on the translator's labors, founded on and supported by my prolonged and intimate contact with her mind—an amalgam of stainless steel rationality and gossamer-silk sensibility.

Of course, Cecile and I often engaged in debate about my poetry. To me it seemed obvious I was no Rilke, no Cavafy, no Auden, but Cecile kept digging for profound meanings under undeniable weaknesses, or the wingless vagueness of some line of mine. She was convinced that these very ambiguities were emitting panic-stricken distress signals. I must confess that whenever Cecile, in her pugnacious prescience, asked me what I meant in this or that line, while I kept whispering "I don't know" or "I don't remember what I had in mind"—that often happens to a poet—she would come up with an extremely appealing interpretation. So identical to what I myself would have offered, I would adopt it without hesitation, neglecting my possible misappropriation of intellectual property.

That's all well and good, but one question remains: upon arrival at that checkpoint, will acceptance expect me or will rejection immediately . . . deport me?

How will I enter Yale, how will I start making noise without a belt packed with explosive values? If they ask me what poetry is, what will I say? "I don't know"? And if they ask me what inspiration is, what will I say? "Who knows"? Will they consider my answers literary or illiterate? Who knows . . .

THE OMNIPOTENCE OF THINGS

Cecile Inglessis Margellos

These pages are translations. From a tongue
That haunts the memory I have become.
  — Yves Bonnefoy

At her induction into the Athens Academy in 2002, Kiki Dimoula—a female poet addressing an audience of men, mostly scholars and scientists—shied away from trying to define concepts, which "only through Art's intervention can undergo a metamorphosis from something known into something unknown in such a way as to offer a pleasant surprise."

Then she launched a metaphor:

"Once, on the road to Alexandroupolis [in Thrace], long before I reached the city, I saw storks' nests, high up, at the tops of a line of telegraph poles.

"Protruding from the poles, the bases of the nests were fluffy and shiny, like the fancy frills that decorate cradles, ready to welcome newborns. In the middle of each nest stood a stork, erect, immobile, on one leg, as if in this ascetic position, in this ciphered balance, it was protecting secrecy's sacred hatchling, already protected from above by the celestial cradle net.

"Poetry is like a nest to hide in. It is built on a pointed height so as to be inaccessible to the rapacious curiosity of anyone who wants to see too clearly what's being hatched inside it. The most efficient way to safeguard concealment is by subtraction. Art is ever-vigilant, elliptical, balancing on one leg. When we write, we subtract."

Playfully intricate as it may be, this metaphor provides more than one thread to lead us through Dimoula's poetic labyrinth. Art is a stork: in order to protect its very common egg-words against base interpretation, it must build its very common nest on uncommonly inaccessible heights. Then it must guard that nest by standing in it, precariously balanced on one leg. Poetry is thus a craft of elevation and concealment, paradoxically reached through curtailment.

Dimoula does not claim that art should keep the hoi polloi at a safe distance. She does imply, however, that a too-conspicuous poetry risks triviality by inviting a univocal reading. What guards against conspicuousness, thereby protecting the poem's diversity of meaning, is elliptical expression. Less is more in poetic ethics, too.

Mystery is therefore paramount to poetry and one way to achieve it is through elevation. Yet contrary to the Longinian sublime, this elevation is not a matter of theme: the poet does not dwell on elevated subjects, motifs, ideas, or words but elevates common — or poeticizes anti-poetical — ones. Through her *alchimie du verbe*, Dimoula transmutes "lower class" things into precious ones, base metals into gold. Even an unremarkable adverb will change rank on the ontological ladder, climbing to a higher level — human or semi-divine:

> To you, *Suddenly*, I appeal.

> Dreamfed *Suddenly*,
> insanely brave, beautiful.
> ["My Last Body"]

"By glorifying what is apparently insignificant, [Dimoula] creates a secret poetic theology of ecumenical ramifications," noted the poet Chistoforos Liontakis.

Hand in hand with this elevation is Dimoula's defamiliarization of the familiar through animistic gestures:

> Today's Friday I'll go to the market square
> to stroll through the decapitated gardens

> to see the aroma of oregano
> enslaved in small bunches.
> ["As If You'd Chosen"]

Her anthropomorphism encompasses objects ("foolish bells"), natural phenomena ("eavesdropping light," "mistrustful green," "irresolute fruit"), bodily functions ("And when we cry, don't listen / to the glands' lie / that supposedly tears wash their hands"), and abstractions ("venomous abundance of opposites," "love-crazed splendor"). Yet this re-enchantment of our "worn-out earth" is counterbalanced by a frequent disenchantment of high and mighty notions. Cardinal concepts—love, death, memory, oblivion, soul, heaven—are violently shaken off their pedestals. "Formerly great significances" undergo a radical demystification and are treated with flippant impertinence. Take Eternity, for instance:

> "Believe me, I'll love you eternally"
> Death repeats every moment
> to Eternity
>
> and moaning
> with miserable certainty
>
> "oh, can't you just lie for once!"
>
> she curses him.
> ["Selective Eternity"]

Dimoula's desacralizing irony does not even spare God:

> Whether or not you were involved in the slip of omnipotence,
> in our terror's ancient
> authentic gospels remains inscribed
> the exorbitant price you demand for your immortality:
> our mortality
> (your great slanderer but also your supporter).
> ["The Unproven Is Innocent"]

She speculates, "Maybe miracles are also mortal." Speculating, or even doubting, however, does not resemble Jacques Derrida's rejection of "the metaphysics of presence," nor does it amount to a total negation. It does not even mirror the primordial Hesiodic Chaos or the abysmal nothingness to which the Greek writer Nikos Dimou referred in his article "In Photography's Square Night" (1990): "Photographs are one of Kiki Dimoula's major themes. How could it be otherwise? Every photograph, be it the humblest, is the presence of an absence. And Dimoula's poetry, as poetry of the nonbeing, always circles around this absence. 'What has died' may not always exist in a photograph, but what exists in a photograph is certainly dead. The instant dies in the instantaneous snapshot."

Indisputably, a photograph is an instant's still life, the printed record of its fleeting light:

> Your photograph stationary.
> You look as if you're on your way
> you smile as if you're not.
> Dried flowers to one side
> ceaselessly repeat
> their unsoiled name *sempervivum*
> *sempervivum* — everlasting, everlasting
> so you won't forget what you are not.
> ["Nonexpectations"]

But does this "presence of absence" really signify an existential or metaphysical void? I would argue that Dimou's oxymoron points in the opposite direction. Instead of a nonbeing, it indicates an excess of being, where absence *itself* becomes a living and acting thing.

In *Camera Lucida*, Roland Barthes discusses photography's mechanical repetition of "what could never be repeated existentially," and the kind of "absented presence" that ensues. Dimoula's photographs accede, for their part, to a higher and fuller existential status. Looking at a photograph produces a sought-after mnemonic effect (let's call it a *voluntarily* involuntary memory), whereby temporal distance is magically abolished. In this new, conflated temporality, absences are substantiated not as ghosts of a new Odyssean *nekyia* but as incarnate companions: "I love photographs," confessed Dimoula in a 2011 interview, "because they give flesh to shadows. And this prevents them from disintegrating and disappearing right away."

Photographs are but one example of Dimoula's vitalism, whose tidal stream fills her poems with animated beings: words, objects, people, feelings (love, unlove, despair, longing, loss), and abstractions (life, old age, decay, time, death, more time, more death, time again). Corporeal or spectral, creatures of language or the stuff of dreams, they are all vividly present. They flood the same space and share the same level of reality (or unreality).

In her own quest for the poetic rose, "absent from all bouquets," Dimoula — unlike Stéphane Mallarmé — becomes an inveterate anti-Platonist: it is not Ideas that are dissimulated by material things but things that are hidden inside Ideas. Her démarche is noticeably akin to that of Yves Bonnefoy, who believes that poetry's role is not to reveal a different or higher reality but to open a (steep) path that leads to it. In fact, Dimoula's stance is metaphysical only if *metaphysical* is not construed as transcending the physical but as following behind it, inferior to it in rank (according to one of the etymologies of the Greek prefix *meta-*).

To the journalist Olga Sella, Dimoula admitted: "Of course I'm a realist, since after every boisterous and vainglorious dream, which first shakes me up and then walks out on me, I always catch myself pompously declaring, *So then things are thus*, as I acknowledge the omnipotence of things."

Not only do these things/beings never completely disappear or die, but they keep exchanging attributes and qualities as if driven by an irresistible metamorphic impulse. This is especially apparent in situations of deep emotional distress, as in the poem "Mother of the Floor Below," which describes her daughter and grandchildren's moving from the family house to a new apartment:

> The moving die's been cast — the upstairs apartment now an
>   empty cube.
>
> Packed into huge cartons the needle and thread that
> sewed offspring footsteps, descendant noises
> to the hem of my reassurance — water, sweet affectionate child,
> running through the night and down
> to me so I could hear it.
>
> Cartons boxes bundles well-secured with the severed
> umbilical cord.
> It was no longer possible no elevator no garage
> especially no extra bath, an entire four-membered excuse —
> the mother is of very old construction.

There is no deliberate carnivalistic reversal in Dimoula's poems. Nor is there a grotesque or scatological aspect, symptomatic of the Rabelaisian novel or satyr drama. Yet the levels between natural and social hierarchies — high and low, lofty and abject — become indistinct. In the baroque construction of her texts, divisions between heterogeneous ontological categories — material and immaterial, profane and sacred, prosaic and lyrical, ominous and comical — disappear. Opposites become interchangeable: humans are reified, abstractions anthropomorphized, nouns adjectivized and adjectives (as well as verbs, adverbs, pronouns, prepositions) nominalized.

Most important, the boundaries between literality and figurality become permeable. For Dimoula's vision of things is neither literal nor metaphoric: it is a unique blend of metaphorized literality and literal metaphoricity — one constantly sliding under the other's skin. As with *leaning*, for instance, in the poem "I Went Through," which undergoes a dual grammatical and figural mutation — the adjectival participle becomes a gerund, while the body's position is transformed into a metaphor for time:

> I received brief postcards:
> a cordial farewell from Patras
> and some regards
> from the Leaning Tower of Pisa.
> No, I'm not sad about the day's leaning.

More revelatory still is the cunning superposition of linguistic, literal, and figural strata in the poem "The Periphrastic Stone"—a title itself bespeaking this accumulation. Here each word is simultaneously a lexical entity, a three-dimensional thing (or being), and a metaphor:

> Say something.
> Say "wave," which won't stand still.
> Say "rowboat," which sinks
> if overloaded with intentions.
> Say "instant,"
> which shouts *help*, it's drowning,
> don't save it,
> say
> "didn't hear a thing."

Dimoula's amalgamating technique is equally accountable for her mordant irony, which infuses absurdity into sturdy pragmatism and imbues tragedy with comedy. For Dimoula is, like all true tragedians, prodigiously funny. Through her corrosive humor, the most melancholy or downright macabre instances dissolve into satire:

> It rains with absolute candor.
> So the sky is not a rumor
> it does exist
> and therefore earth is not
> the sole solution

as each lazy dead person pretends.
["Untitled"]

The corollary is self-mockery—a constant trait. Dimoula displays an acute knowledge of human nature, her own first and foremost:

Whatever you tell the pen, it writes.
You think remember suppose love dictate.

. . . .

Sometimes when the pen lets the cold in
because precautions warp
due to the age of the hardships,
you distort the image slightly—
turning a feeling that reaps bitter winter
into one that plucks chamomiles
and so the text's weather grows milder.
["Painful Revelation"]

The professor and poet Nasos Vagenas rightly noted this paradoxical intermingling of lyricism and irony in Dimoula's self-referential verse: "Qualifying irony as 'lyrical' is in itself ironic, for it constitutes a contradiction in terms: irony (contemplating things from a distance) is the opposite of lyricism (expressing a personal feeling born from within)."

Thus, from stanza to stanza, Dimoula's extraordinary and extraordinarily moving poetry transforms our way of seeing. Our most stereotypical realities undergo a metamorphosis—or, better still, an anamorphosis, the distortion of perspective so dear to Renaissance painters. While absence becomes steel, "tears' words get completely lost," and a childhood trauma "grows teeth hair crooked nails knives," we start seeing "the skull beneath the skin"—as does Webster in T. S. Eliot's "Whispers of Immortality." But on that same skull we also detect a frolicsome or deeply compassionate smile.

Nikos Dimou shrewdly observed that J. A. Cuddon's description of the seventeenth-century English metaphysicals (Donne, Herbert,

Marvell) applies as well to Dimoula: "Arresting and original images and conceits (showing a preoccupation with analogies between macrocosm and microcosm), wit, ingenuity, dexterous use of colloquial speech, considerable flexibility of rhythm and meter, complex themes (both sacred and profane), a liking for paradox and dialectical argument, a direct manner, a caustic humour, a keenly felt awareness of mortality, and a distinguished capacity for elliptical thought and tersely compact expression." If we add the unorthodox, indeed heretical, use of the Greek language, the strangled syntax, and the delight in neologisms, this constitutes a fine synopsis of Dimoula's poetics.

But one could equally relate Dimoula's anticlassical aesthetics to the art of French baroque poets such as Théophile de Viau, Tristan L'Hermite, Saint-Amant, and Étienne Durant. Her verse is redolent of their asymmetries, dialectical arguments, paradoxes, and techniques of illusionism and chiaroscuro. The American Emily Dickinson's grammatical heterodoxy, undercut transcendentalism, and anticlimactic irony are also kindred. As are Wisława Szymborska's earthbound animism and satire-ridden morbidity. (An example of similarity in theme and tonality is the portrayal of death in Szymborska's "On Death, Without Exaggeration": "It can't even get the things done / that are part of its trade: / dig a grave, / make a coffin, / clean up after itself," from *The People on the Bridge*, translated by Stanisław Barańczak and Clare Cavanagh.) Moreover, the notable kinship in ontological approach between Dimoula's and Yves Bonnefoy's poetic stances is worth stressing (compare the similar treatment of the photograph motif in Dimoula's "Photograph 1948" and "Montage" and Bonnefoy's "A Photograph" and "Another Photograph," translated by Hoyt Rogers in *Second Simplicity: New Poetry and Prose, 1991–2011*.)

Of all the aspects of her craft, however, Dimoula clearly prefers to underscore the formal ones. In 2007, two poets, Antonis Fostieris and Thanassis Niarchos, asked her: "In your poems one usually senses an absence, a lack, a paradise lost—whether these relate to a person, an age in life, an object, or a situation. Is poetry, necessarily, the satisfaction of a privation, the consolation for a misfortune, the healing of a wound?" Typically, Dimoula skirted her interviewers' focus on biographical or psychological content to stress the importance of language: "In addition to all the things you enumerate, which are undoubtedly true, there also exists a special, secretive time whose only concern is to cultivate the future of language, its euphonic use, its functional relation to subtraction, its co-habitation with allusion—in short, to cultivate this mysterious *how*: how it is possible that, even though all has been said, language insists and persuades us that the most important things still remain unsaid."

Here we can detect Dimoula's concern—indeed, her anxiety—to mitigate the impression that her poetry is primarily descriptive, narrative, or didactic. We feel her need to shift the emphasis from the semantic to the linguistic aspects of her work, from the signified to the signifier. She insists that a poem is also a matter of form and structure—a text is *texture*. Poetic diction, says Dimoula, requires euphony—by which she means a prosaic and sometimes dissonant musicality rather than a consonant melodiousness. But most of all, it requires mystery and allusion, which in turn demand subtraction—which takes us back to the one-legged stork.

But if subtraction is a key element in Dimoula's poetic architecture, of what kind is it? It is not lexical minimalism, for her vocabulary is anything but spare. Dimoula's poetic stance first centers around structure, or rather a destructured restructuring. On all levels: lexical, grammatical, syntactic, and semantic.

Critics invoke musical parallels, comparing her poems' form to that of a fugue, the only term "capable of describing the variety and wealth of contrapuntal combinations that we come across in her work" (Yiorgos Yottis). Others compare her poetry to pop art (Jannis Psychopedis) or define it as "surrealism of grammar and syntax" (Tasos Roussos). I believe that analytic cubism is an even more appropriate pictorial analogue: multifaceted objects, fusion of planes, nonlinear perspective, spatio-temporal simultaneity. An architectural correlate would be deconstructivism. Frank Gehry's irregular shapes and iconoclastic, dynamic geometry come to mind.

There is no doubt that Dimoula's structure dispenses with linguistic armature, grammatical pillars, syntactic pegs, morphological and logical supports, lexical symmetries and semantic articulations. Her compact synthesis relies on reduction, shortcutting, and elimination. The mysterious "ciphered balance" she evokes derives from an initial imbalance, prompted by a technique of destabilization. For Dimoula believes that access to a new or regained meaning, to a *sens retrouvé*, is possible only if poetic utterance (certainly *her* poetic utterance) loses its foothold and is thereby forced to seek a new, delicate yet firm equilibrium.

It is a truism that in literature, especially in poetry, content is inextricably linked to form, and that the latter is inseparable from the structure of the language it employs. This makes translation of poetry—"where even the order of the words is a mystery" (to borrow Saint Jerome's adage about the sacred scriptures)—an arduous task.

To translate even the most conventional or prosaic line of poetry from Greek into English, one must come to grips with the crippling and sometimes forbidding differences between the two language structures. Contrary to English, Greek is a gendered and pronoun-dropping language. It is also a highly inflected one—an aspect that allows a relatively free-ordered syntax. Inevitably, these inherent formal and structural features affect the outcome of English translations from Greek both semantically and stylistically.

The fact that Greek nouns (as well as pronouns, adjectives, participles, and articles) possess genders (feminine, masculine, and neuter) greatly facilitates allegorizing. Take, for instance, the first lines of Dimoula's "Selective Eternity": "'Believe me, I'll love you eternally' / Death repeats every moment / to Eternity." In Greek, "death" (θάνατος) is masculine, whereas "eternity" (αἰωνιότητα) is feminine. Not only are the two abstractions automatically personifiable because of their genders, but their belonging to opposite "sexes" makes their "love affair" all the more obvious. In our genderless English rendition, the allegorical aspect was dealt with by the capitalization of both nouns and by making Eternity a "she" in the last line. Still, the playing-out of this parodic courtship between two de facto genderless abstractions makes less immediate sense to the English reader.

The lack of gender in English affects even this volume's title: *The Brazen Plagiarist*. It is taken from the title of a brilliant self-referential poem about writing, personified as a "brazen unholy plagiarist." In Greek, "writing" (γραφή) is feminine. It is by no means inconsequential that the word shares the writer's own gender—that, thereby, the craft is identified with the craftswoman, the poetic deed with the poet herself. From the translator's point of view, the semantic loss is of no little importance. Had the title been in Greek, the existential undertones of the coincidence of genders would have instantly come into sharp relief.

Additionally, inferable pronouns may be omitted in Greek, whereas English sentences require a subject. In English translations, the repetition of a subject before each verb, especially in poems written in the first person (frequent in Dimoula's corpus), is visually and rhythmically disruptive. In our rendition of "I Went Through," for instance, the first-person subject pronoun "I" (totally absent in the Greek) is repeated no less than thirty-eight times, twenty-three of them at the beginning of the line:

I take a walk and night falls.
I make a decision and night falls.
No, I'm not sad.

I've been curious and studious.
I know things. Something about everything.

Another substantial difference between the two languages: in the Greek language, the relations among parts of speech are clearly defined by their inflections. This allows a very free word order. (Of course Dimoula goes farther still, dispensing with punctuation and articles, largely resorting to figures of speech — anacolutha, asyndeta, hyperbata, enjambment, and so on — in short, breaking the norms of even this very loose syntactic order.) Conversely, in English, grammatical and syntactic relations are indicated by a more or less determined position of the words in the sentence, and, additionally, by pronouns, prepositions, auxiliaries, particles, and other markers. Moreover, Greek can be made even more compact by its wide variety (even the ad hoc creation) of compound words. Thus, the analytical English phrasing often struggles to mirror the density of the Greek. To give but one example, in the first stanza of "The Finder's Reward," the English translation, laconic as it strives to be, contains nine more words than the source text:

> Thumbing through, you hesitated now and then
> in your reading, as if something had got to you,
> unread, the pages were secretly laughing.

> Τὰ ξεφύλλιζες, κοντοστεκόσουν κάθε τόσο
> διάβαζες τάχα κάτι σὲ διαπερνοῦσε
> ἀδιάβαστες κρυφογελοῦσαν οἱ σελίδες.

The most economical translations my co-translator and I could come up with for these lines' subject-free, one-word Greek verbs demanded a minimum of two words each: "thumbing through" (ξεφύλλιζες), "you hesitated" (κοντοστεκόσουν), "had got to" (διαπερνοῦσε), "were secretly laughing" (κρυφογελοῦσαν).

An emblematic poem in the present volume epitomizes and metaphorizes the Greek language's formal characteristics, intermingling poetic and meta-poetic, figural and pragmatic dimensions within a

single conceit. It reflects on the meaning of meaning-ridden words —
love, fear, memory, night — via their grammatical definitions.

> Love:
> noun, substantive,
> extremely substantive,
> singular in number;
> gender not feminine, not masculine,
> gender defenseless.
> Plural the number
> of defenseless loves.
>
> Fear:
> substantive,
> singular to start with
> plural afterward:
> fears.
> Fears of
> everything from now on.
> ["The Plural"]

A side note: In Greek grammatical reality, as in traditional allegorical imagery, "love" (*eros*) is masculine. But in Dimoula's personal mythology it can be claimed by neither gender — and certainly not by the neuter!

If dealing with the conventional morphological and structural features of Greek prose is a challenge for even the most seasoned translator, translating Dimoula's unconventional, deconstructed, and unorthodox idiom into English is indeed a tall order. No wonder so few English translations of this major poet have seen the light until now. With two notable exceptions — David Connolly's publication of forty-six poems in 1996, and Olga Broumas' twenty-poem Web site publication in 2011 — only a few translations of Dimoula's

poems can be found, scattered throughout various English antholo-
gies of Greek poetry. True as it may be that "impossible things in
translation are those that haven't been done" (David Bellos), Dimou-
la's translators—especially into English—bend under the weight of
what I would nonetheless call near-impossibilities.

These challenges were exponentially multiplied for the present
translation, for it was the product of collaboration between two trans-
lators, geographically, biographically, and even culturally oceans
apart: Rika Lesser, an accomplished American poet and translator
of Swedish and German poetry, who spoke not a word of Greek;
and me, a Greek literary translator into and from Greek, ancient
Greek, and French, whose English was precarious. Obvious ques-
tions arise: Why use *two* translators and why us? The reason behind
this venturesome choice was my firmly held conviction that trans-
lating Dimoula's poetry demanded qualities hard to find in a single
translator: a native speaker's immersion in both languages and their
cultural heritages (something quite impossible unless you are Nabo-
kov), solid translational and poetic ability, a transcendent belief in
and an incandescent passion for translation, and a zealot's faith in
Dimoula's poetic genius.

I assumed (perhaps presumptuously) that I possessed certain of
these qualities—devotion to and understanding of Dimoula's oeuvre
above all. Before I decided to embark body and soul on this trans-
lation, I ran some comparative tests: much to my surprise, where I
read ἀρειμάνιος πλοῦτος as "chain-smoking wealth," for example,
experienced translation wordsmiths had read it as "bellicose wealth"
(trusting the adjective's etymology of the word), "opulent wealth," or
"panache's wealth." To me, these were misinterpretations indicative
of the difficulty (for a non-native speaker of Greek, especially) in fol-
lowing the arcane evolution of a word's meaning from ancient to con-
temporary, colloquial Greek. Dimoula's command and subtle use of
these changes of signification were even more difficult to apprehend.

But in taking on this translation, I also knew that I lacked other qualities—mastery of English (let alone of poetic English), first and foremost. It was therefore evident that a talented co-translator was needed. Jennifer Banks, my insightful editor at Yale University Press, was certain that Rika Lesser was the ideal person. It was she who put the two of us into contact and encouraged us to undertake this translation in tandem.

Of course, there were risks, drawbacks, sometimes insurmountable obstacles, and virulent disputes. Dimoula's Greek is ingeniously un-Greek. Preserving her idiosyncrasies qua idiosyncrasies in English was, in turn, an acrobatic exercise. Rendering her misuse—even abuse—of vocabulary, grammar, and syntax, re-creating her sparkling wordplay, conveying her syncretic idiom with its surprising interweaving of a demotic vernacular and an archaic or formal, mandarin, Greek required a juggler's skill.

Normalization, standardization, homogenization were never far away, at least at the beginning, when my co-translator must have thought that I was either totally unschooled in English or a dogmatic literalist, or both. But even later, the temptation to standardize had to be kept on a tight leash, if only because, as David Bellos posits, "Translators are instinctively averse to the risk of being taken for less than fully cultivated writers of their target tongue." The urge to correct lexical incongruities, put one-legged grammar back on its two feet, smooth out semantic asperities—in short, to "better" Dimoula's Greek in English—kept coming back like a return of the repressed, against a deeper feeling that what Walter Benjamin calls "the incomprehensible, the secret, the 'poetic'" ought to be preserved.

Since this is meant to be an introduction, not a monograph, I will focus on a few areas in which Dimoula's stylistic mannerisms caused us permanent headaches: nominalizations, adjectivizations, and neologisms.

Nominalizations are probably the most striking trait in Dimoula's idiom, detectable even in many of her book titles: *The Little of the World, Hail Never, A Moment of Two, Sound of Distancings.* Dimoula will nominalize (reifying or personifying) just about everything: a conventional greeting: "we sat on the same *good morning* / and gazed at nature" ("good morning" translates the single word καλημέρα, which is far simpler to turn into a noun than the two-word English greeting). An exclamation: "I thought of throwing a blossoming Amen." A verb: "the *it-happened-so*" (the verb is ἔτυχε; the unavoidable addition of the personal pronoun "it" gave our compound verb an even less nounlike aspect; thus adding italics and hyphens was the only solution). A preposition: "the withouts have changed" (the plural is as strange in Greek as it is in English; we kept it). A pronoun: "Identical to That, just like twins. / I, however, am far more afraid of This." An adverb: "The supine rows best." (We started off by cautiously normalizing: "Rowing supine is simplest." But Rika — who was gradually "turning Kikian" — agreed to risk a bolder rendition.) An adjective: "Unfruitfuls" (an uncountable adjective transformed into a countable noun; we could not but singularize it, and it became "Unfruitful").

Nominalized adjectives were a conundrum. They are relatively common in Greek and uncountably many in Dimoula's verse, but rare in English. In many cases, we had to resort to various imperfect solutions depending on the context: capitalization (the Known, the Unknown, the Inexplicable), italics ("that *irrevocable* / that prunes us"), reformulation by a relative clause ("And winds that uproot what is stagnant"), a gerund ("ripening"). But most often we would use an abstract noun, a solution that resulted in a semantic deviation, if not necessarily a clear loss. Abstract nouns, such as *bitterness, recurrence,* or *pointlessness,* are not the exact semantic equivalents of their corresponding nominalized adjectives: *the bitter, the recurrent, the pointless.* The Greek decoding brain construes the former as allegories but understands the latter as pointedly instantiated things or beings. On the poet's stage, they become concrete objects or living actors — all fully participating in her play.

Since in Dimoula's poetry everything is interchangeable, the corollary to nominalization is adjectivization, whereby beings or incorporeal entities become qualities or attributes. In "Oblivion's Adolescence," for instance, a gaze qualifies a thread: "With eyesight thread I stitch in place / the silver buttons of Distance." Our "eyesight" translates Dimoula's neologistic adjective βλεμμάτινη: "gazy" or "made of gaze." Keeping the adjectival form in English was no easy task (we had also considered "sightliney" at some point). Nor were this poem's other translators any luckier—"thread of sight," "gazing's thread," "my look like a thread" all seemed even weaker.

With Dimoula's neologisms, we were indeed on very slippery ground. "Pre-hangman" (a title) was not much of a dilemma, since it was a match to Dimoula's equally invented Προ–Δήμιος. Nor was the epithet "Godfallen" ("To you, Godfallen / small-bodied Time"), which imitated the neologism Θεοκατέβατε—Dimoula's brilliant coinage after the existing compound word ουρανοκατέβατος, "sky-fallen."

Conversely, "Charonography" did not come easily. It is used to translate Χαρογραφία (Charography), an invented compound forged from Χάρος (Charon, the ferryman of Hades) and the suffix –γραφία ("-graphy")—probably an ironic wordplay with the quasi-homophone χορογραφία (choreography). In the eerie atmosphere of this poem about a visit to a drugstore in which poison phials are on display, Dimoula's neologism was impressively apposite.

The greatest controversy, though, occurred over "Nonexpectations"—our final translation of Ἀπροσδοκίες—a hard-won, last minute victory of "Nonexpectations" over both "Unexpectations" and "Non-expectations." Ἀπροσδοκίες is a poem title, repeated within the poem, and paired with the equally incongruous, extremely rare ἀγνωρισιά (nonrecognition). The crux of the matter was mainly the following lines, in which the speaker speculates on the chances of an encounter in the afterlife, while looking at her deceased companion's photograph:

No news from you.
Your photograph stationary.
As it rains without raining.

As a shadow returns a body to me.
And as we will meet up there
one day.
In some barrens overgrown
with shady nonexpectations
and evergreen circumlocutions.

We argued over this forever, Rika insisting upon "non-expectations" (mostly on grounds of linguistic incongruity), I refusing to budge from "unexpectations." My reasons for opposing her were (a) morphological: "unexpectations" looked more like a *word* than the hyphenated "non-expectations"; (b) stylistic: I was convinced that ἀπροσδοκίες was Dimoula's creation, typical of her inclination toward neologism, and that it should therefore be treated accordingly and matched with an analogous, however bizarre, neologism in English; (c) semantic, most of all: I assumed that it had stemmed from the existing adjective ἀπροσδόκητο (unexpected). Since "unexpected" is perforce something unforeseeably realized, this inconceivable encounter did not seem so inconceivable after all. I had therefore reached the conclusion that, contrary to "non-expectations," with or without a hyphen, the Greek word revealed a secret hope for an otherwordly happy ending; in other words, I had willfully endowed it with positive undertones.

Well, I was wrong. The word, though unknown to Dimoula, and a hapax legomenon (it is to be found only in Speusippus's Platonic *Terms*), is *unexpectedly* extant. And it indisputably means "nonexpectations" as the opposite of "expectations." Once more, Dimoula was being bitterly ironic, and I refused to see it. This was clearly what one would call a hermeneutical bias (or, to put it bluntly, pure wishful thinking): there would never be raining without rain; no shadow would ever return "a body to me" (behind this "me" hides the poet, the reader, and this most assiduous of readers, the translator).

Hats off to Rika Lesser, whose poetic instinct outdid both my knowledge of Greek and my unconscious wish for an improbable, unhoped-for resurrection.

It is in translation's honor that this fervent quest for a *meaningful* re-instantiation of meaning never ceased, and that it will certainly go on long after we hand this manuscript to the press. For I cannot but agree with George Steiner's ethical stance: "To re-create what has been created so as to affirm, to enunciate its primacy, its seniority of essence and existence, to re-create it in ways which add presentness to presence, which *ful-fil* that which is already complete: this is the purpose of responsible translation."

Kiki Dimoula's corpus up to 2010 encompasses more than four hundred poems, only about a hundred of which meet with her unequivocal approval. In making the selection for this volume, we felt that her preferences had to be respected, not only in deference to her wishes but also because they were a guide to what she herself considers worthy and most representative of her style. But we had other criteria. Quantity was an important issue—the book was to be bilingual, so there were space limitations. Translatability and readability also mattered. There are poems which are clearly not transposable to another language—the self-referential poems, in particular, whose subject is language itself, and where the signifier *is* the signified. Representativeness was a third. As this is the first comprehensive English translation of a wide selection of poems from across Dimoula's oeuvre, it was important to include poems illustrative of each phase of her work. Two early poems Dimoula had discarded were therefore added: "Melancholy" and "British Museum," from her first collection, *Erebus*. We also decided to include some beautiful poems that were inexplicably missing from the poet's personal canon, such as "Montage" and "Common Fate" (*The Little of the World*), "Substitute" (*Hail Never*), and "Be Careful" (*We've Moved Next Door*). While these were added, others were abandoned for various reasons in the course of translation. Seventy-nine poems is our grand total (it could have been eighty, had not one of us believed that nine was her lucky number!). They are the product of two years' struggling, jubilating, fighting, discreetly crying, and loudly laughing. We offer them to our English readers with pride and gratitude.

The rest is poetry.

THE SOMATICS OF SEMANTICS
THE BODY OF THE WORK
Rika Lesser

What does it mean, to "know" a language? to "read" someone's poetry? to "encounter great poetry"? And to recognize, or be cognizant of the fact that you have?

> Draw a word out of the night
> at random.
> An entire night at random.
> Don't say "entire,"
> say "tiny,"
> which releases you.
> Tiny
> sensation,
> entire
> sadness
> all mine.
> An entire night.

Who would not be moved by the lapidary words above, a fragment chipped from "The Periphrastic Stone," included in Kiki Dimoula's 1971 breakthrough volume *The Little of the World*? Who would not feel their weight, their gravity, and be impressed by them? Or by these longer lines from "Lower Class," a poem inspired by her visit to the sanctuary of Olympia, which appeared in *Oblivion's Adolescence*, 1994:

Disproportion's civilizations and tombs
are topsy-turvy in my mind.
I forget in which of their annihilations
so many illustrious dates made their camps,
when power was proclaimed the ultimate goal,
I always confuse whatever happened prior to my existence
with as-if-it-hadn't-happened. After we cease to exist
mark my words
my confusion will prove prophetic.

I better comprehend
the stones scattered all around
as they were, anonymous, brought to light by the excavation,
parts of some wholeness —
no one knows which lower level
of earth it went under.
To me their lost meaning is familiar.
I comfort them by inscribing them
as the branches' faint movements inscribe
the scattered spring air.

The coincidence of weight and lightness, stillness and movement, presence and absence, time and space is uniquely Dimoula, while her discriminations, how she draws her boundaries, is eerily familiar. Compare Dimoula's "I always confuse whatever happened prior to my existence / with as-if-it-hadn't-happened" from the poem above with Rilke's "Not that you were frightened when you died, / nor that your strong death interrupted us / in darkness, tearing the Until-then from the Up-till-now" from his "Requiem for a Friend" for Paula Modersohn-Becker, written in 1908.

I would like to lie down on the floor with the poems of Kiki Dimoula. I have *learned to (re)write* streaming through me in all directions at once — in Greek and in English, in the poet's voice (which I have heard only in recordings), in my own, in the voice of my co-translator (which I have heard live and recorded), all of which play in my head, have been playing in my head, since May 2010.

We learn by experience and experimentation, somatically as much as intellectually incorporating all we have attempted in our successes and failures. We can improve our skills and our lives if we allow ourselves to go on exploring, with curiosity, in a state of neutral and attentive open-mindedness. Call it negative capability. In this context I will call it "translator's brain holding various lingual possibilities simultaneously, spherically, and weighing them, undecided, in one or more languages under consideration." It is that moment in Paradise of sensing and feeling, before—in suspension of—judgment. A state of potentiality before action is taken. We train, in literature as in life, in many different ways, to be prepared to move, to take action in any direction at any time, as needed. Survival depends on it.

> Whatever you tell the pen, it writes.
> You think remember suppose love dictate.
>
> Some things you pass over in silence.
> ["Painful Revelation"]

My imperfect knowledge of Kiki Dimoula's work I will pass over in silence. An account of how I came to translate her work follows.

It is no secret, or an open one, that I have long been opposed to translating poetry from languages one does not "know." For years I have spoken and written about translating and reading poets in translation, of having counted myself part of a dying breed of American Poet-Translators Who Translate Only from Languages They Know Intimately (or Extremely Well), and, while not predominantly scholars, who have no fear of scholarship. These are people for whom the translation of poetry is every bit as creative and essential to their "practice" as writing their own poems. This is fundamentally different from the practice of Scholars (American or not) Who Translate

Poetry, who tell you everything about the original poems, even how to sound out the original texts, but do not show you, do not provide you with poems that are a pleasure to read in English.

An American poet who grew up speaking only English but eager to learn other languages, I feel as closely related to Rilke—my first real love in another language—as I do to Dickinson. I may feel closer to Gunnar Ekelöf than to Pound. I have felt asymptotically close to Göran Sonnevi, whose work I have translated for more than twenty-five years, whose single long poem extends through all his books, whose language encompasses literature, science, philosophy, politics, and music. And I am just as near a relation of "Walt Whitman, an American, one of the roughs, a kosmos," who walked these Brooklyn streets before me.

When approached about translating Kiki Dimoula's poetry, many signals in my neurologically American system sounded alarms; lights went off and on, and on. Life knows no stasis. Over time many things had changed. Chief in my own biography and biology, after several years' practice of tai chi chuan, I had begun to train as a *Feldenkrais* practitioner (an educational training often described as somatic). In waking life, sensitive to change, aware of locomotion, I move and breathe with a pulse, think rhythmically, cyclically, use language, work with language when necessary, when expedient. Writing poetry—nearly a lifelong practice for me—is a necessity. My intention? Life, with pleasure. As Wallace Stevens wrote to Henry Church, the man to whom he dedicated *Notes Toward a Supreme Fiction*, "the essence of poetry is change and the essence of change is that it gives pleasure."

The request came on May 3, 2010, from Jennifer Banks, who had been my editor on Sonnevi's *Mozart's Third Brain*. She wrote of Kiki Dimoula as an "astounding Greek poet"; she and Cecile Inglessis Margellos were looking for someone to serve as Cecile's co-translator. I trusted her judgment—not my lack of Greek—because Jennifer had recognized Sonnevi's "greatness"; her instincts and enthusiasm helped me find him a home at Yale. It was not long before Cecile and I began our transoceanic work.

> Because you associate
> with suspect worlds
> —especially that of the soul—
> someday you'll be summoned by the police
> for interrogation, identification.

> Be careful
> your confession
> must be terse.
> ["I Do Not Know"]

Even before I began to learn the Greek alphabet, a twisted ball of Greek roots was available to me in the thesaurus at the base of English, howsoever confused as they wend through Latin or French. I knew from the first that the only way I could proceed was to attend to the poems read aloud. I had played the piano and studied voice in my youth and, as I have written elsewhere, had a quarter century of experience working with Göran Sonnevi's voice. I learned early and by heart that the center of the mind and the soul is the body.

Fortunately there is a Greek compact disc on which quite a few of the poems in this selection are recorded. Kiki Dimoula's voice is deep and dark, as is my co-translator's. Cecile recorded and sent me MP3 files of the remaining poems, spoken at normal rates and more slowly, so that I could hear the poems properly as well as follow every word on each page.

At first I received translations of the poems that hewed as closely to the Greek lineation as possible in addition to transcriptions of the Greek texts into the English alphabet, with interlinear word-for-word approximations. (At this point my recognition of Greek letters was limited to what I knew from chemistry and calculus.) Once I had learned the Greek alphabet, Cecile continued to supplement her English drafts of the poems with something like word-for-word keys. But I also became proficient at keyboarding the poems, word by word, into Google-translate onscreen while listening to the recordings. The Google translations were dumbfounding, beyond oracular. But I needed to hear and feel and see the word boundaries as well as get the sense (semantic) and sensation (auditory and rhythmic) of every separate word.

I would also listen repeatedly to the poems in Greek while looking at the Greek text, marking it in pencil and colored markers—on photocopies rather than in the books—until I could distinguish all the words, hear similarities, repetitions. I needed to get the sense (semantic) and sensation (auditory and rhythmic) of the phrasing of the words in the sentences.

My co-translator and I exchanged countless drafts via e-mail, and we discussed poems—sometimes for hours on end—using Skype from variable locations. We would read versions to each other back and forth, discuss allusions, idioms, synonyms, etymologies, mutual misunderstandings, occasional successes. I printed out many drafts and marked the printouts. We discussed every word and line in detail, maddening for both of us.

Just after Hurricane Irene left New York on August 28, 2011, I left for Greece, and we worked together for a week or so, revisiting all we had done up until then—some forty-five poems—and going forward a bit. Between late September and late December, we worked even more intensively on the remaining thirty-four. Drafts of another handful or two were cast off along the way.

I have read other translations of Kiki Dimoula, not all that exist in all the languages I can read. Time was certainly a constraint—the desire to produce a book during the poet's lifetime. But it also became clear to me, as time went on and my understanding of Dimoula's *corpus* improved and deepened, and as I continued to consult various French and Swedish translations, that indeed Cecile Inglessis Margellos is the most exacting, the most devoted, the most faithful of

Dimoula's readers. We are all in her debt for bringing Kiki Dimoula to us. Without her intelligence, the poet's voice would still be dark smoky background music I might dance to.

Who now is the marionette and who pulls the strings? It gives me great joy once again lightly to tap out these words in these lines *translated* from the title poem of the poet's most recent volume, *The Finder's Reward*, 2010:

> unread, the pages were secretly laughing
>
> then you weighed them all in the palm of your hand
> as if they were coins
> and made a rough estimate
> not so few, you said,
> surprised, how did you come by them, you asked me.
>
> Hypocrite, you haven't read a single line
> or else you would have seen
> it's the first thing I wrote
>
> they're the finder's reward
> you gave them to me
> because I found you
> . . . .
> I didn't subtract a single one
> of the thousand beauties you possessed
> nor one speck of your precious ugliness
> World.

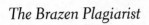

The Brazen Plagiarist

Ποιήματα (1998)

Poems (1998)

ΕΡΕΒΟΣ (1956)

.

EREBUS (1956)

ΜΕΛΑΓΧΟΛΙΑ

Στὸν οὐρανὸ ἀκροβατεῖ μεγάλη σκοτεινιά.

Κι ἔτσι καθὼς μὲ πῆρε τὸ παράθυρο ἀγκαλιά,
μὲ τὸ ἕνα χέρι
στὸ δωμάτιο μέσα σέρνω
τοῦ δρόμου τὴν ἀπίστευτη ἐρημιά,
μὲ τὸ ἄλλο παίρνω
μιὰ χούφτα συννεφιὰ
καὶ στὴν ψυχή μου σπέρνω.

MELANCHOLY

In the sky heavy darkness walks a tightrope.
And as the window takes me into its embrace,
with one of my hands
into the room I drag
the street's inconceivable barrenness,
while with the other one I grab
a handful of cloudmist
and with it seed my soul.

ΒΡΕΤΑΝΙΚΟ ΜΟΥΣΕΙΟ

ΕΛΓΙΝΟΥ ΜΑΡΜΑΡΑ

Στὴν ψυχρὴ τοῦ Μουσείου αἴθουσα
τὴν κλεμμένη, ὡραία, κοιτῶ
μοναχὴ Καρυάτιδα.
Τὸ σκοτεινὸ γλυκύ της βλέμμα
ἐπίμονα ἐστραμμένο ἔχει
στὸ σφριγηλὸ τοῦ Διονύσου σῶμα
(σὲ στάση ἡδυπαθείας σμιλευμένο)
ποὺ δυὸ βήματα μόνον ἀπέχει.
Τὸ βλέμμα τὸ δικό του ἔχει πέσει
στὴ δυνατὴ τῆς κόρης μέση.
Πολυετὲς εἰδύλλιον ὑποπτεύομαι
τοὺς δυὸ αὐτοὺς νά 'χει ἑνώσει.

Κι ἔτσι, ὅταν τὸ βράδυ ἡ αἴθουσα ἀδειάζει
ἀπ' τοὺς πολλούς, τοὺς θορυβώδεις ἐπισκέπτες,
τὸν Διόνυσο φαντάζομαι
προσεκτικὰ ἀπ' τὴ θέση του νὰ ἐγείρεται
τῶν διπλανῶν γλυπτῶν καὶ ἀγαλμάτων
τὴν ὑποψία μὴν κινήσει,
κι ὅλος παλμὸ νὰ σύρεται
τὴ συστολὴ τῆς Καρυάτιδας
μὲ οἶνον καὶ μὲ χάδια νὰ λυγίσει.

Δὲν ἀποκλείεται ὅμως ἔξω νά 'χω πέσει.
Μιὰν ἄλλη σχέση ἴσως νὰ τοὺς δένει
πιὸ δυνατή, πιὸ πονεμένη:
Τὶς χειμωνιάτικες βραδιὲς

BRITISH MUSEUM
THE ELGIN MARBLES

In the chill of the Museum room
before my eyes: stolen, fair
sole Caryatid.
Her dark sweet gaze
persistently fixed
on Dionysos' robust body
(sculpted in a posture of lust)
just two steps away.
His own gaze has fallen
on the girl's strapping waist.
An everlasting idyll
unites them, I suspect.
And so, in the evening, when the room empties
out the many, noisy visitors,
I imagine Dionysos
carefully rising from his stand
arousing no suspicion among
neighboring statues and sculpted stones,
vibrantly slithering
to undo the Caryatid's chastity
with wine and with caresses.

Maybe I'm wrong.
Some other tie may bind them
more strongly, more woefully:
On wintery evenings

καὶ τὶς ἐξαίσιες τοῦ Αὐγούστου νύχτες
τοὺς βλέπω,
ἀπ' τὰ ψηλὰ νὰ κατεβαίνουν βάθρα τους,
τῆς μέρας ἀποβάλλοντας τὸ τυπικό τους ὕφος,
μὲ νοσταλγίας στεναγμοὺς καὶ δάκρυα
τοὺς Παρθενῶνες καὶ τὰ Ἐρεχθεῖα ποὺ στερήθηκαν
στὴ μνήμη τους μὲ πάθος ν' ἀνεγείρουν.

and splendid August nights
I see them
stepping down from their pedestals,
discarding their formal daytime miens,
and with nostalgia's sighs and tears
erecting passionately in memory
Parthenons and Erechtheions they've lost.

ΕΡΗΜΗΝ (1958)

IN ABSENTIA (1958)

ΟΥΤΟΠΙΕΣ

Καθ᾿ ὁδὸν,
(7 καὶ 30´ πρωινὴ πρὸς ἐργασίαν)
συναντῶ τὸν Μάρτιο
εὐδιάθετον,
ὑπαινιγμῶν πλήρη
περὶ ἀνοίξεως καὶ λοιπά.

Ἀναβάλλω τὴν ὑπόστασή μου,
ἀνακόπτω τὴ σύμβασή μου
μὲ τὸ χειμώνα,
καὶ διασπείρομαι σὲ χῶμα.
Μιὰ μικρὴ γῆ φυσικὴ συντελοῦμαι,
ξαπλωμένη, ἁπλωμένη
ἀπέναντι στὸ
καθ᾿ ὅλα σύμφωνο
σύμπαν.

Φυτεύομαι ἄνθη,
ἀνθίζω συναισθήματα,
καὶ εἶμαι πολὺ καλὰ
εἰς ἄπλετον προορισμὸν
καὶ τοποθέτησιν.

«Ἀπαγορεύεται ἡ ἄνοιξις!»
ξάφνου μιὰ πινακίδα — σύννεφο
ἀπειλεῖ. Ἀμέσως
μιὰ βροχὴ ἄρχισε κι ἔλεγε
εἰς βάρος τῆς ἀνοίξεως

UTOPIAS

On my way
into work, 7:30 A.M.
I encounter March—
cheerful,
hinting broadly
about spring and so forth.

I postpone my essential nature,
break my contract
with winter,
and strew myself as humus over the ground.
I become a small plot of earth,
lying outstretched
facing
a wholly sympathetic
universe.
I plant myself with flowers,
blossom with feelings,
and feel very well
within my boundless destination
and position.

"Spring Prohibited!"
suddenly a sign—a cloud—
threatens. At once
a downpour starts speaking
accusing spring

καὶ εἰς βάρος μου,
ἕνας δύσθυμος ἄνεμος
μοῦ κατάσχει τὰ ἄνθη,
μοῦ κατάσχει τὰ συναισθήματα
καὶ μ' ὁδηγεῖ στὸ Γραφεῖο.

Παράβασις, λοιπόν, βαρεία,
καὶ μάλιστα καθ' ὁδόν,
ἀπὸ κυρία σχεδὸν ὥριμη,
μὲ οἰκογενειακὲς ὑποχρεώσεις,
καὶ πολυετὴ θητείαν
εἰς Δημόσιαν θέσιν
καὶ χειμῶνες.

and accusing me,
a black-browed wind
seizes my flowers
seizes my emotions
and forces me to the Office.

A serious transgression, then
—and on her way in—
by a woman of a certain age,
who has family obligations
and many years of service
to the public
and to winter.

ΜΕΤΑΘΕΣΙΣ

Ἡ νύχτα ἐνταφιάζει ἀθόρυβα
στὸν τύμβο τῆς σιωπῆς της
τὸ σῶμα τῆς ἡμέρας,
τῆς μάνας τῶν ἔργων μου.

Κι ἐγώ, τὰ ὀρφανὰ κι ἀνήλικα
τοῦτα ἔργα μου
μαζεύω γύρω μου,
καὶ τὰ προετοιμάζω
γιὰ τὴν ἄγνωστη μητριά τους:
τὴν αὐριανὴν ἡμέρα.

TRANSFER

Night quietly buries
in its tomb of silence
today's body,
mother of my works.

And I, around myself,
I gather orphans and minors,
these works of mine,
getting them ready
for their unknown stepmother:
the day to come.

ΑΣΥΜΒΙΒΑΣΤΑ

Ὅλα τὰ ποιήματά μου γιὰ τὴν ἄνοιξη
ἀτέλειωτα μένουν.

Φταίει ποὺ πάντα βιάζεται ἡ ἄνοιξη,
φταίει ποὺ πάντα ἀργεῖ ἡ διάθεσή μου.

Γι᾽ αὐτὸ ἀναγκάζομαι
κάθε σχεδὸν ποίημά μου γιὰ τὴν ἄνοιξη
μὲ μιὰ ἐποχὴ φθινοπώρου
ν᾽ ἀποτελειώνω.

INCOMPATIBLES

All my poems about spring
remain incomplete.

Spring is always in a hurry,
my mood always long delayed.

That's why I'm compelled
to complete
almost every poem I write about spring
with an autumn season.

ΡΟΜΑΝΤΙΚΗ ΔΙΑΦΩΝΙΑ

Καὶ βέβαια εἶμαι
κατὰ τῆς διαταράξεως τῆς σελήνης.
Οἱ λόγοι πολλοί.
Ἐκτὸς ἀπ' τὴν κακόσχημην ὑπερβολὴ
—ἐγὼ ἀπὸ καιρὸ τὶς ἀποφεύγω
λόγω ὑπερκοπώσεως—
εἶναι καὶ ἀπρέπεια.
Οἱ σχέσεις της μὲ τὴ γῆ
ὑπῆρξαν ἕως τώρα
ἄκρως τυπικές.
Διακριτικὴ μὲς στὴ μαγευτικὴ ἀπόστασή της,
ἔδωσε λύσεις ἄψογες
στῆς ἀνθρωπότητας τὴ ρέμβη.
Καί, τὸ κυριότερο,
δωρεὰν κάθε τόσο
αὐτὴ τὴν ἐφθαρμένη γῆ
ἐπαργυρώνει.

ROMANTIC DISAGREEMENT

Of course I am
against disturbing the moon.
For many reasons.
Not only is it an unseemly exaggeration
—personally I've long avoided exaggerating
because of exhaustion—
but it is also improper.
So far, the moon's relations with the earth
have been
highly formal.
Discreet from its enchanting distance,
it offered perfect solutions
to mankind's musing.
And, above all,
every so often,
it silver-plates
this worn-out earth for free.

ΕΠΙ ΤΑ ΙΧΝΗ (1963)

ON THE TRACK (1963)

ΔΥΟ ΜΙΚΡΑ ΠΟΙΗΜΑΤΑ

ΓΙΑ ΕΝΑ ΑΙΝΙΓΜΑ ΚΑΙ ΕΝΑ ΔΡΟΜΟ

I

Γιὰ σένα στὶς ἐπιθυμίες μου
λόγος δὲν ἔγινε ποτέ.
Δὲν σὲ προέβλεψαν ποτὲ
τὰ ὄνειρά μου.
Οἱ προαισθήσεις μου
δὲν σὲ συνάντησαν.
Οὔτε ἡ φαντασία μου.
                          Κι ὅμως
μιὰ ἀνεξακρίβωτη στιγμὴ
σ᾽ ἐξακριβώνω μέσα μου
ἕνα ἕτοιμο κιόλας αἴσθημα.

II

Πλατιὰ ποὺ ἦταν ἡ Σταδίου
καθὼς χωροῦσε
τὸ μεσημέρι τὸ εὔχυμο,
τὸν ἀνδρισμό σου,
καὶ μένα
βαδίζοντας πλάι σου
σὲ ἀπόσταση
μιᾶς ὁλόκληρης θλίψης.

TWO SHORT POEMS
FOR A RIDDLE AND A STREET

I

My desires were never
told about you.
You were never predicted
by my dreams.
My premonitions
haven't met you.
Nor has my imagination.

                 And yet
for an indeterminate moment
I determine that you're inside me:
a feeling already ready.

II

So vast was Stadiou Street
with room enough
for succulent noon,
your virility,
and me
walking beside you
one whole sadness
apart.

ΒΙΟΓΡΑΦΙΚΟΣ ΠΙΝΑΚΑΣ

Στὴ μάνα μου

Τὸ σπίτι
κοιτάζει τὸν δημόσιο δρόμο
καὶ τὴ θάλασσα
μὲ λογικὴ τεσσάρων παραθύρων,
χαμογελώντας στερεότυπα
μ' ἕνα πλατὺ πορτοκαλὶ
μπαλκόνι.

Σ' αὐτὸ τὸ μπαλκόνι
σ' αὐτὸ τὸ χαμόγελο
τ' ἀπογεύματα, ἡ μάνα μου
τὸ δυσανάγνωστό της πρόσωπο
ἐκθέτει.

Ὁ χρόνος τὸ συνέγραψε
χωρὶς ἔξαρση
ἀπὸ νύχτα σὲ νύχτα
σὲ γλώσσα πόνου ῥέουσα
γεμίζοντας
κατεβατὰ φθορᾶς.
Κι οὔτε ἕνα λάθος γέλιου.

Κάθεται
ἄκρη ἄκρη στὴν καρέκλα
νὰ μὴν ἐπιβαρύνει τὸ ἀπόγευμα

BIOGRAPHICAL PICTURE

To my mother

The house
looks at the public road
and the sea
by the logic of its four windows,
smiling stereotypically
with a wide orange
balcony.

On this balcony
on this smile
each and every afternoon, my mother
exposes
her indecipherable face.

Time wrote it down
with no excitement
night after night
in pain's fluid language
filling
page after page of decay.
And without one mistake of laughter.

She sits
on the edge of the chair
not to burden the afternoon

μ' ὅλο τὸ βάρος τῆς κατάκοιτης καρδιᾶς της,
ἴσα ἴσα νὰ ὑπάρχει
σταματημένη μέσα στὴ ζωή της
ἀπὸ μιὰν ἄπνοια τύχης,
ἴσα ἴσα γιὰ ν' ἀντέξει τώρα
τῆς ἔκπληξής της τὸ σπασμό:

«Ὑπάρχουν θάλασσες
καράβια νευρικὰ
ποὺ σπρώχνουν λύσεις
στὸ ἀνεμπόδιστο;
Καὶ ἄνεμοι ποὺ ξεριζώνουνε τὰ στάσιμα;
Κι αὐτὰ τὰ εὔληπτα ποὺ πίνει χρώματα
τὸ ἀλκοολικὸ ἀπόγευμα
ὑπάρχουν;» Δὲν τό 'ξερε.
Δὲν τό 'ξερε ἡ ζωή της.

Τώρα
ἀποτολμᾶ μιὰ κίνηση παράξενη:
λίγο τὸ σῶμα ῥίχνει ἐμπρός,
τὸ ξαναφέρνει πίσω,
βαριὰ κωπηλασία μνήμης κάνει,
γιαλὸ γιαλὸ τὰ δάκρυά της.

Σιγὰ σιγὰ
ἀπόγευμα, πρόσωπο καὶ μπαλκόνι
ἀπὸ τὸ σούρουπο ὑποσκάπτονται.
Τὸ σχῆμα τους παραφρονεῖ.

with the full weight of her bedridden heart,
just to exist
stopped in the midst of her life
by some dead calm of luck,
just to bear
the spasm of her surprise:

"Are there seas,
nervous ships
that push solutions
toward unhindrance?
And winds that uproot what is stagnant?
And these colors, easy to absorb,
which the alcoholic afternoon imbibes—
do they exist?" She didn't know.
Her life didn't know.

Now
she risks a strange movement:
she thrusts her body slightly forward,
and then pulls it back—
heavy rowing of memory—
her tears go shore by shore.

Little by little
the afternoon, her face and the balcony
are undermined by twilight.
Their shape grows insane.

Σὲ χῶρο θάμπους κλείνονται
νὰ μὴν μποροῦν νὰ μποῦν ἄλλο τὰ μάτια μας.
Νυχτώνει.

Συκιά, καλοκαίρι 1961

They themselves get shut up in dusk
our eyes can no longer enter.
Night is falling.

Sykia, Summer 1961

ΠΑΣΧΑ, ΠΡΟΣ ΣΟΥΝΙΟΝ

Ἡ θάλασσα ψύχραιμη καὶ ἀσύσπαστη,
λὲς κι ἀπ' τὶς ἄκρες της σφιχτὰ
τὴν ἔπιασ' ἡ στεριὰ καὶ τὴν τεντώνει.
Στὴν ἄκρη τοῦ γκρεμοῦ,
ποὺ συγκρατεῖ τὸ θέαμα,
εὐωδιάζει ὁ ἴλιγγος
κατρακυλοῦν αὐτοκτονίες...

Ἀριστερά, ἡ ἐποχή,
σὲ μιὰ ἀκατάσχετη ἐπιφοίτηση χρωμάτων.
Κι ἐκεῖ, προσκυνητάρι κατηφές,
ἕναν Χριστό, μὴ ἀναστάντα προφανῶς, ἐγκλείει.
Γιατὶ στεφάνι ἐκ πλαστικοῦ
ἐπάνω του ἀκόμη ξεχασμένο
τὸ πάθος τῆς Σταυρώσεως παρατείνει.

Περὶ διαγενομένου τοῦ Σαββάτου,
Μαγδαληνῆς, Σαλώμης, καὶ ἀρωμάτων
ἰδέαν δὲν ἔχει.

Σύμπτωσις:
Κι ἀπ' τὴν καρδιά μου ὁ λίθος
οὐκ ἀποκεκύλισται·
ἦν γὰρ μέγας σφόδρα.

EASTER, TOWARD SOUNION

The sea, unperturbed and untwitching
as if the land clutches it tightly
by the edges, pulls and stretches.
At the edge of the cliff
propping up the view,
vertigo smells sweet
suicides tumble . . .

To the left, the season,
in an irrepressible descent of holy color.
And right there, a gloomy shrine
encloses a Christ, apparently unrisen.
For on him a plastic wreath
still forgotten
prolongs the passion of the Cross.
Concerning *the Sabbath that was past,*
Magdalene, Salome, and the spices
there's no clue.
Coincidence:
from my heart, too, the stone
was not *rolled away:*
for it was very great.

ΤΟ ΛΙΓΟ ΤΟΥ ΚΟΣΜΟΥ (1971)

THE LITTLE OF THE WORLD (1971)

ΠΕΡΑΣΑ

Because these wings are no longer wings to fly.
—T. S. Eliot

Περπατῶ καὶ νυχτώνει.
Ἀποφασίζω καὶ νυχτώνει.
Ὄχι, δὲν εἶμαι λυπημένη.

Ὑπῆρξα περίεργη καὶ μελετηρή.
Ξέρω ἀπ' ὅλα. Λίγο ἀπ' ὅλα.
Τὰ ὀνόματα τῶν λουλουδιῶν ὅταν μαραίνονται,
πότε πρασινίζουν οἱ λέξεις καὶ πότε κρυώνουμε.
Πόσο εὔκολα γυρίζει ἡ κλειδαριὰ τῶν αἰσθημάτων
μ' ἕνα ὁποιοδήποτε κλειδὶ τῆς λησμονιᾶς.
Ὄχι, δὲν εἶμαι λυπημένη.

Πέρασα μέρες μὲ βροχή,
ἐντάθηκα πίσω ἀπ' αὐτὸ
τὸ συρματόπλεγμα τὸ ὑδάτινο
ὑπομονετικὰ κι ἀπαρατήρητα,
ὅπως ὁ πόνος τῶν δέντρων
ὅταν τὸ ὕστατο φύλλο τοὺς φεύγει
κι ὅπως ὁ φόβος τῶν γενναίων.
Ὄχι, δὲν εἶμαι λυπημένη.

Πέρασα ἀπὸ κήπους, στάθηκα σὲ συντριβάνια
καὶ εἶδα πολλὰ ἀγαλματίδια νὰ γελοῦν
σὲ ἀθέατα αἴτια χαρᾶς.
Καὶ μικροὺς ἐρωτιδεῖς, καυχησιάρηδες.

I WENT THROUGH

Because these wings are no longer wings to fly.
  —T. S. Eliot

I take a walk and night falls.
I make a decision and night falls.
No, I'm not sad.

I've been curious and studious.
I know things. Something about everything.
The names of flowers when they fade,
and when words grow green and when we grow cold.
How readily the lock of feelings unlocks
with any of oblivion's keys.
No, I'm not sad.

I went through days of rain,
surging behind
the liquid barbed wire
patiently and discreetly,
like pain in the trees
when the last leaf leaves them,
and like fear in the brave.
No, I'm not sad.

I went through gardens, stood at fountains,
saw many statuettes laughing
at invisible causes of joy.
And boastful little Cupids.

Τὰ τεντωμένα τόξα τους
βγήκανε μισοφέγγαρο σὲ νύχτες μου καὶ ρέμβασα.
Εἶδα πολλὰ καὶ ὡραῖα ὄνειρα
καὶ εἶδα νὰ ξεχνιέμαι.
Ὄχι, δὲν εἶμαι λυπημένη.

Περπάτησα πολὺ στὰ αἰσθήματα,
τὰ δικά μου καὶ τῶν ἄλλων,
κι ἔμενε πάντα χῶρος ἀνάμεσά τους
νὰ περάσει ὁ πλατὺς χρόνος.
Πέρασα ἀπὸ ταχυδρομεῖα καὶ ξαναπέρασα.
Ἔγραψα γράμματα καὶ ξαναέγραψα
καὶ στὸ θεὸ τῆς ἀπαντήσεως προσευχήθηκα ἄκοπα.
Ἔλαβα κάρτες σύντομες:
ἐγκάρδιο ἀποχαιρετιστήριο ἀπὸ τὴν Πάτρα
καὶ κάτι χαιρετίσματα
ἀπὸ τὸν Πύργο τῆς Πίζας ποὺ γέρνει.
Ὄχι, δὲν εἶμαι λυπημένη ποὺ γέρνει ἡ μέρα.

Μίλησα πολύ. Στοὺς ἀνθρώπους,
στοὺς φανοστάτες, στὶς φωτογραφίες.
Καὶ πολὺ στὶς ἁλυσίδες.
Ἔμαθα νὰ διαβάζω χέρια
καὶ νὰ χάνω χέρια.
Ὄχι, δὲν εἶμαι λυπημένη.

Ταξίδεψα μάλιστα.
Πῆγα κι ἀπὸ δῶ, πῆγα κι ἀπὸ κεῖ...
Παντοῦ ἕτοιμος νὰ γεράσει ὁ κόσμος.

Their stretched bows rose as
half-moons in my nights, and I was lost in reveries.
I dreamed many a lovely dream
and went on daydreaming.
No, I'm not sad.

I walked around a lot in feelings,
mine and those of others,
and there was always space between them
for wide time to pass.
I went by post offices and went by again.
I wrote letters and wrote again
and tirelessly prayed to the god of answers.
I received brief postcards:
a cordial farewell from Patras
and some regards
from the Leaning Tower of Pisa.
No, I'm not sad about the day's leaning.

I talked a lot. To people,
to lampposts, to photographs.
And a great deal to chains.
I learned how to read palms,
how to lose hands.
No, I'm not sad.

I've even traveled.
I went this way, and I went that way . . .
Everywhere, the world was ready to get old.

Ἔχασα κι ἀπὸ δῶ, ἔχασα κι ἀπὸ κεῖ.
Κι ἀπὸ τὴν προσοχή μου μέσα ἔχασα
κι ἀπ' τὴν ἀπροσεξία μου.
Πῆγα καὶ στὴ θάλασσα.
Μοῦ ὀφειλόταν ἕνα πλάτος. Πὲς πὼς τὸ πῆρα.
Φοβήθηκα τὴ μοναξιὰ
καὶ φαντάστηκα ἀνθρώπους.
Τοὺς εἶδα νὰ πέφτουν
ἀπ' τὸ χέρι μιᾶς ἤσυχης σκόνης,
ποὺ διέτρεχε μιὰν ἡλιαχτίδα
κι ἄλλους ἀπὸ τὸν ἦχο μιᾶς καμπάνας ἐλάχιστης.
Καὶ ἠχήθηκα σὲ κωδωνοκρουσίες
ὀρθόδοξης ἐρημίας.
Ὄχι, δὲν εἶμαι λυπημένη.

Ἔπιασα καὶ φωτιὰ καὶ σιγοκάηκα.
Καὶ δὲν μοῦ 'λειψε οὔτε τῶν φεγγαριῶν ἡ πεῖρα.
Ἡ χάση τους πάνω ἀπὸ θάλασσες κι ἀπὸ μάτια,
σκοτεινή, μὲ ἀκόνισε.
Ὄχι, δὲν εἶμαι λυπημένη.

Ὅσο μπόρεσα ἔφερ' ἀντίσταση σ' αὐτὸ τὸ ποτάμι
ὅταν εἶχε νερὸ πολύ, νὰ μὴ μὲ πάρει,
κι ὅσο ἦταν δυνατὸν φαντάστηκα νερὸ
στὰ ξεροπόταμα
καὶ παρασύρθηκα.

Ὄχι, δὲν εἶμαι λυπημένη.
Σὲ σωστὴ ὥρα νυχτώνει.

I lost this way, and I lost that way.
Lost something of my attentiveness
and of my inattentiveness.
I also went to the sea.
I was owed some breadth. Let's say I got it.
I feared loneliness
and I imagined people.
I saw them drop
from the hand of some tranquil dust
that moved through a sunbeam.
And others from the tinkling of a tiny bell.
I resounded in the chiming
of orthodox wilderness.
No, I'm not sad.

I also caught fire and was slowly consumed.
I shared the moons' experience.
Their waning, over seas and eyes,
into the dark, has sharpened me.
No, I'm not sad.

As much as I could I resisted this river
at high water, not to be carried off.
And as much as possible I imagined water
in dry riverbeds
and went adrift.

No, I'm not sad.
The night falls right on time.

Ο ΠΛΗΘΥΝΤΙΚΟΣ ΑΡΙΘΜΟΣ

Ὁ ἔρωτας,
ὄνομα οὐσιαστικόν,
πολὺ οὐσιαστικόν,
ἑνικοῦ ἀριθμοῦ,
γένους οὔτε θηλυκοῦ οὔτε ἀρσενικοῦ,
γένους ἀνυπεράσπιστου.
Πληθυντικὸς ἀριθμὸς
οἱ ἀνυπεράσπιστοι ἔρωτες.

Ὁ φόβος,
ὄνομα οὐσιαστικόν,
στὴν ἀρχὴ ἑνικὸς ἀριθμὸς
καὶ μετὰ πληθυντικός:
οἱ φόβοι.
Οἱ φόβοι
γιὰ ὅλα ἀπὸ δῶ καὶ πέρα.

Ἡ μνήμη,
κύριο ὄνομα τῶν θλίψεων,
ἑνικοῦ ἀριθμοῦ,
μόνον ἑνικοῦ ἀριθμοῦ
καὶ ἄκλιτη.
Ἡ μνήμη, ἡ μνήμη, ἡ μνήμη.

Ἡ νύχτα,
ὄνομα οὐσιαστικόν,
γένους θηλυκοῦ,

THE PLURAL

Love:
noun, substantive,
extremely substantive,
singular in number;
gender not feminine, not masculine,
gender defenseless.
Plural the number
of defenseless loves.

Fear:
substantive,
singular to start with
plural afterward:
fears.
Fears of
everything from now on.

Memory:
noun, proper name for sorrows,
singular in number,
singular only,
and indeclinable.
Memory, memory, memory.

Night:
substantive,
gender feminine,

ἑνικὸς ἀριθμός.

Πληθυντικὸς ἀριθμὸς
οἱ νύχτες.

Οἱ νύχτες ἀπὸ δῶ καὶ πέρα.

number singular.
Plural in number
the nights.
The nights from now on.

ΖΟΥΓΚΛΑ

Πρωὶ κι ὅλα τοῦ κόσμου
στημένα
στὴν ἰδεώδη ἀπόσταση μιᾶς μονομαχίας.
Τὰ ὅπλα ἔχουν διαλεχτεῖ,
τὰ ἴδια πάντα,
οἱ ἀνάγκες σου, οἱ ἀνάγκες μου.
Αὐτὸς ποὺ θὰ μέτραγε ἕνα, δύο, τρία, πῦρ
καθυστεροῦσε,
κι ὥσπου νὰ ᾿ρθεῖ
καθίσαμε στὴν ἴδια καλημέρα
καὶ χαζεύαμε τὴ φύση.

Ἡ ἐξοχὴ βρισκότανε στὴν ἥβη
καὶ τὸ πράσινο ἀσελγοῦσε.
Κραυγὲς τροπαιοφόρου θηριωδίας
ἔσερνε ὁ Ἰούνιος τῆς ὑπαίθρου.
Πιανόταν καὶ πηδοῦσε
ἀπὸ κλαδὶ δέντρων κι αἰσθήσεων
σὲ κλαδὶ δέντρων κι αἰσθήσεων,
Ταρζὰν ταινίας μικροῦ μήκους
ποὺ κυνηγάει ἀθέατα θηρία
στὴ μικρὴ ζούγκλα μιᾶς ἱστορίας.
Τὸ δάσος ὑποσχότανε πουλιὰ
καὶ φίδια.
Δηλητηριώδης ἀφθονία ἀντιθέτων.
Τὸ φῶς ἔπεφτε καταπέλτης
σ᾿ ὅ,τι δὲν ἦταν φῶς,

JUNGLE

Morning and all things in the world
are positioned
at ideal distance for a duel.
Weapons have been chosen,
always the same,
your needs, my needs.
The man who counts *one, two, three, fire*
was delayed,
and while awaiting his arrival
we sat on the same *good morning*
and gazed at nature.

The countryside was pubescent,
the verdure lecherous.
Open-air June screamed and cried
with triumphant cruelty.
It hung and jumped
from tree limbs and senses
to tree limbs and senses,
like Tarzan in a short film
hunting invisible beasts
through a tale's small jungle.
The forest promised birds
and serpents.
A venomous abundance of opposites.
Light was catapulted
onto what was not light,

κι ἡ ἐρωτομανὴς λαμπρότης
παράφορα φιλοῦσε κι ὅ,τι δὲν ἦταν ἔρωτας,
μέχρι καὶ τὴ δική σου συνοφρύωσι.

Στὴ μικρὴ ἐκκλησία ἄλλος κανεὶς
ἐκτὸς ἀπὸ τὸ πολὺ ὄνομά της, Ἐλευθερώτρια.

Ἕνας Χριστὸς περίφροντις
μέτραγε μὲ τὸ πάθος τοῦ φιλάργυρου
τὸ βιός του:
καρφιὰ κι ἀγκάθια.

Ἐπόμενο ἦταν νὰ μὴν ἔχει ἀκούσει
τοὺς πυροβολισμούς.

and the love-crazed splendor
also ardently kissed what was not love
even your own surliness.

In the small church nothing
but its solemn name, *Liberator.*
A zealous Christ
with a miser's passion counted
his riches:
nails and thorns.
No wonder he didn't hear
the shots.

ΣΗΜΕΙΟ ΑΝΑΓΝΩΡΙΣΕΩΣ

ΑΓΑΛΜΑ ΓΥΝΑΙΚΑΣ ΜΕ ΔΕΜΕΝΑ ΤΑ ΧΕΡΙΑ

Ὅλοι σὲ λένε κατευθείαν ἄγαλμα,
ἐγὼ σὲ προσφωνῶ γυναίκα κατευθείαν.

Στολίζεις κάποιο πάρκο.
Ἀπὸ μακριὰ ἐξαπατᾶς.
Θαρρεῖ κανεὶς πὼς ἔχεις ἐλαφρὰ ἀνακαθίσει
νὰ θυμηθεῖς ἕνα ὡραῖο ὄνειρο ποὺ εἶδες,
πὼς παίρνεις φόρα νὰ τὸ ζήσεις.
Ἀπὸ κοντὰ ξεκαθαρίζει τ᾽ ὄνειρο:
δεμένα εἶναι πισθάγκωνα τὰ χέρια σου
μ᾽ ἕνα σχοινὶ μαρμάρινο
κι ἡ στάση σου εἶναι ἡ θέλησή σου
κάτι νὰ σὲ βοηθήσει νὰ ξεφύγεις
τὴν ἀγωνία τοῦ αἰχμάλωτου.
Ἔτσι σὲ παραγγείλανε στὸ γλύπτη:
αἰχμάλωτη.
Δὲν μπορεῖς
οὔτε μιὰ βροχὴ νὰ ζυγίσεις στὸ χέρι σου,
οὔτε μιὰ ἐλαφριὰ μαργαρίτα.
Δεμένα εἶναι τὰ χέρια σου.

Καὶ δὲν εἶν᾽ τὸ μάρμαρο μόνο ὁ Ἄργος.
Ἂν κάτι πήγαινε ν᾽ ἀλλάξει
στὴν πορεία τῶν μαρμάρων,
ἂν ἄρχιζαν τ᾽ ἀγάλματα ἀγῶνες
γιὰ ἐλευθερίες καὶ ἰσότητες,

IDENTIFICATION MARK

STATUE OF A WOMAN WITH TIED HANDS

People call you statue straight away,
straight away I call you woman.

You adorn a park.
From a distance you deceive our eyes.
We think you are about to rise
as you recall a lovely dream you had
and push off to live it.
Close up the dream grows clear:
your hands are tied behind you
with a rope of marble,
and your posture is your desire
for something to help you escape
the agony of the captive.
Such was the demand placed on the sculptor:
a captive.
You cannot
weigh rain in your hand,
not even a light daisy.
Your hands are tied.

It's not just the marble that guards you like Argus.
If something were to change
in the progression of marbles,
if statues would start fighting
for freedom and equality,

ὅπως οἱ δοῦλοι,
οἱ νεκροὶ
καὶ τὸ αἴσθημά μας,
ἐσὺ θὰ πορευόσουνα
μὲς στὴν κοσμογονία τῶν μαρμάρων
μὲ δεμένα πάλι τὰ χέρια, αἰχμάλωτη.

Ὅλοι σὲ λένε κατευθείαν ἄγαλμα,
ἐγὼ σὲ λέω γυναίκα ἀμέσως.
Ὄχι γιατὶ γυναίκα σὲ παράδωσε
στὸ μάρμαρο ὁ γλύπτης
κι ὑπόσχονται οἱ γοφοί σου
εὐγονία ἀγαλμάτων,
καλὴ σοδειὰ ἀκινησίας.
Γιὰ τὰ δεμένα χέρια σου, ποὺ ἔχεις
ὅσους πολλοὺς αἰῶνες σὲ γνωρίζω,
σὲ λέω γυναίκα.

Σὲ λέω γυναίκα
γιατ' εἶσ' αἰχμάλωτη.

like the slaves,
the dead,
and our feelings,
you would progress
through the cosmogony of marbles
again with hands tied, captive.

People call you statue straight away,
I immediately call you woman.
Not because the sculptor turned you over
to the marble as a woman
or because your hips promise
a multitude of statues,
a fine harvest of immobility.
For the tied hands you've had
through all the centuries I've known you,
I call you woman.

I call you woman
because you are captive.

ΦΩΤΟΓΡΑΦΙΑ 1948

Κρατῶ λουλούδι μᾶλλον.
Παράξενο.
Φαίνετ' ἀπ' τὴ ζωή μου
πέρασε κῆπος κάποτε.

Στὸ ἄλλο χέρι
κρατῶ πέτρα.
Μὲ χάρι καὶ ἔπαρσι.
Ὑπόνοια καμιὰ
ὅτι προειδοποιοῦμαι γι' ἀλλοιώσεις,
προγεύομαι ἄμυνες.
Φαίνετ' ἀπ' τὴ ζωή μου
πέρασε ἄγνοια κάποτε.

Χαμογελῶ.
Ἡ καμπύλη τοῦ χαμόγελου,
τὸ κοῖλο αὐτῆς τῆς διαθέσεως,
μοιάζει μὲ τόξο καλὰ τεντωμένο,
ἔτοιμο.
Φαίνετ' ἀπ' τὴ ζωή μου
πέρασε στόχος κάποτε.
Καὶ προδιάθεσι νίκης.

Τὸ βλέμμα βυθισμένο
στὸ προπατορικὸ ἁμάρτημα:
τὸν ἀπαγορευμένο καρπὸ
τῆς προσδοκίας γεύεται.

PHOTOGRAPH 1948

I'm probably holding a flower.
Strange.
A garden must have gone
through my life once.

In my other hand
I hold a stone.
With grace and defiance.
No hint whatsoever,
no forewarning of changes,
no foretaste of defenses.
Ignorance must have gone
through my life once.

I'm smiling.
The curve of the smile,
the hollowness of this mood,
resembles a well-stretched bow,
ready.
A target must have gone
through my life once.
And a penchant for victory.

My gaze, sunk deep
in original sin,
tastes the forbidden fruit
of expectation.

Φαίνετ᾽ ἀπ᾽ τὴ ζωή μου
πέρασε πίστη κάποτε.

Ἡ σκιά μου, παιχνίδι τοῦ ἥλιου μόνο.
Φοράει στολὴ δισταγμοῦ.
Δὲν ἔχει ἀκόμα προφθάσει νὰ εἶναι
σύντροφός μου ἢ καταδότης.
Φαίνετ᾽ ἀπ᾽ τὴ ζωή μου
πέρασ᾽ ἐπάρκεια κάποτε.

Σὺ δὲν φαίνεσαι.

Ὅμως γιὰ νὰ ὑπάρχει γκρεμὸς στὸ τοπίο,
γιὰ νά ᾽χω σταθεῖ στὴν ἄκρη του
κρατώντας λουλούδι
καὶ χαμογελώντας,
θὰ πεῖ πὼς ὅπου νά ᾽ναι ἔρχεσαι.
Φαίνετ᾽ ἀπ᾽ τὴ ζωή μου
ζωὴ πέρασε κάποτε.

Faith must have gone
through my life once.

My shadow, the sun's mere toy,
wears hesitation's uniform.
It hasn't yet had time to become
my companion or my traitor.
Sufficiency must have gone
through my life once.

You are not there.
But since there's a cliff in the landscape,
and I'm standing at its edge
holding a flower
and smiling,
you must be coming soon.
A life must have gone
through my life once.

MONTAZ

ΦΩΤΟΓΡΑΦΙΑ

Σημεῖο διαχωριστικὸ δύο ἀπεράντων εἶσαι.
Δύο ἀντιμέτωπων πελάγων.
Ὁ οὐρανὸς κι ἡ θάλασσα.
Τὸ πλάτος καὶ τῶν δύο
ἀθροίζεται στὸ μέτωπό σου.
Ἔχεις πλατὺ μέτωπο
ἀντιμέτωπο στὰ ὅρια.
Τὰ δεμένα πανιὰ τῆς μορφῆς σου,
ἡ σκεπτική της πλώρη,
δείχνουν πῶς περιμένεις τρικυμία
τῶν ἀπεράντων.

Ὅμως ἐσὺ κρατᾶς τιμόνι.
Ἐξάρτημα καϊκιοῦ εἶναι
ἢ τῆς ζωῆς σου;
Δική σου εἶναι ἡ βάρκα
ἢ κλεμμένη;
Δικό σου εἶναι τὸ θάρρος
ἢ τῆς φωτογραφίας;
Ὁδηγεῖς ἢ ὁδηγεῖσαι;
Ὑπῆρχε ἀπὸ τὴν ἀρχὴ τιμόνι
ἢ ἔκανε μοντὰζ ὁ φωτογράφος
κι ἀπόκτησε τιμόνι
τὸ ἀκυβέρνητο,
ὅπως βρεθῆκαν οἱ ἀγρότες οἱ παπποῦδες μας
στὰ κάδρα
μὲ γραβάτα;

MONTAGE
PHOTOGRAPH

You're the dividing point between two immensities.
Two confronting seas:
ocean and sky.
The breadth of both
is summed on your forehead.
A wide forehead
that confronts the limits.
The furled sails of your figure
its worried prow
show you expect a storm
of immensities.

But you're at the helm.
Is this a feature of the caïque
or of your life?
Is the boat yours
or stolen?
Is the courage yours
or the photograph's?
Are you steering or being steered?
Was there a wheel from the start
or did the photographer
in his montage add a wheel
to the unsteerable
just as our farmer grandfathers
in framed photographs
were once provided with neckties?

ΤΟ ΛΙΓΟ ΤΟΥ ΚΟΣΜΟΥ

ΦΩΤΟΓΡΑΦΙΑ ΧΕΡΙΟΥ

Ἐδῶ, ἀπέφυγες τὴν περιπέτεια
νὰ ξαναϋπάρχεις
κι εἶναι τὸ χέρι σου μόνο
στὴν τετράγωνη νύχτα τῆς φωτογραφίας.
Σὰν ἀνάσταση σκίζει τὸ χάρτινο σύμπαν
μοναχὸ κι ἀνεβαίνει,
σὰν αἴφνης
ποὺ αἴρει τὸ Λίγο τοῦ κόσμου.
Μὲ τέσσερα ἐπὶ τέσσερα οὐρανὸ ποῦ ξεκινάει;
Ἀλλ᾽ εἶναι ἡ ἀσφυξία τῶν διαστάσεων
ὁ σπόρος τῶν θαυμάτων.

Περιστρέφω τὴ φωτογραφία,
γιατὶ προκαλεῖ ἐθισμὸ
ἡ παρατεταμένη χρήση τῶν θαυμάτων.
Ἐδῶ μοιάζει χέρι
ποὺ κόπηκε ἀπὸ σῶμα χορευτοῦ
τὴν ὥρα ποὺ ἔλεγε ὤπα,
γιατὶ ἄλλη στροφὴ θὰ ἑτοίμαζε ἡ ψυχὴ
κι ἄλλη θὰ μπόρεσε τὸ σῶμα.
Ἀντίρροπος ρυθμὸς ποὺ σπάζει
τὸ μέλος
καὶ τὰ μέλη.

Περιστρέφω τὴ φωτογραφία.
Χέρι ποὺ βαδίζει

THE LITTLE OF THE WORLD
PHOTOGRAPH OF A HAND

Here, you have avoided the risk
of re-existing
and only your hand shows
in the photograph's square night.
Like a resurrection, it tears up the paper universe
alone, and rises
like a *suddenly*
that taketh away the Little of the world.
In a four-by-four sky, where is it heading?
But the suffocation of dimensions
is indeed the seed of miracles.

I rotate the photograph
because the prolonged use of miracles
is addictive.
Here, it looks like a hand
severed from the body of a dancer
the moment he was saying *opa!*
for his soul wanted to turn one way
and his body would allow only the other.
A contrapuntal rhythm that breaks
melodic lines
and limbs.

I rotate the photograph.
A hand walking

στὸν ἥσυχο στενόμακρο Σεπτέμβρη
τῶν πολλῶν καὶ βουβῶν ἀληθειῶν.

Ἐδῶ, τὸ χέρι ποὺ θὰ χάραξε
ἕνα καλὴ ἀντάμωση
στὴν πρώτη πέτρα τῶν ἀνθρώπων.
Εὐχὴ ποὺ πιάνει ἂν φυτευτεῖ
σὲ γῆ φωτογραφίας μόνο.

Μὲ μιὰ ἐλάχιστη κίνηση
τὸ χέρι ἀλλάζει πάλι
ἐπαγγελίες αἰωρήσεως.
Τώρα, ὅμοιο μὲ χάδι ἀνοδικὸ
στὰ μακρινὰ μαλλιὰ μιᾶς μνήμης.

Ἄχ, τί θὰ τὶς κάνει τόσες ὁμοιότητες
γι᾿ αὐτὸν τὸν ἕνα κόσμο;

Ἀφήνω τὴ φωτογραφία νὰ πέσει.
Καὶ τὸ χέρι σου μένει
παλάμη ἀνεστραμμένη
σὲ κάποια χειρομάντισσα νεφέλη,
ποὺ τὸ διαβάζει:
μαζί του δὲν βλέπει νὰ μὲ δένει
καμιὰ συνεργασία στὰ βάρη.
Μαζὶ δὲν θὰ σηκώσουμε
μήτε νεκρὸν ἀπὸ κάτω
μήτε λουλούδι.

on the hushed narrow September
of numerous and silent truths.

Here, the hand that must have scratched
a *see you soon*
on mankind's first stone.
A wish to be realized only if planted
in the soil of a photograph.

With a small gesture
the hand again changes
its promises of levitation.
Now it's like a caress brushing upward,
stroking the distant hair of a memory.

Ah, why does it need all these likenesses
in this one single world?

I let the photograph fall.
And your hand remains
palm up toward
some fortune-telling cloud
that reads it:
no link between me and your hand
through sharing of burdens.
Together we will not raise up
a dead man from the ground
a flower from the soil.

ΤΟ ΔΙΑΖΕΥΚΤΙΚΟΝ Ἢ

Μ' ἔκλεισε μέσα ἡ βροχὴ
καὶ μένω τώρα νὰ ἐξαρτιέμαι ἀπὸ σταγόνες.

Ὅμως ποῦ ξέρω ἂν αὐτὸ εἶναι βροχὴ
ἢ δάκρυα ἀπὸ τὸν μέσα οὐρανὸ μιᾶς μνήμης;
Μεγάλωσα πολὺ γιὰ νὰ ὀνομάζω
τὰ φαινόμενα χωρὶς ἐπιφύλαξη,
αὐτὸ βροχή, αὐτὸ δάκρυα.

Στεγνὴ στέκομαι ἀνάμεσα
στὰ δύο ἐνδεχόμενα: βροχὴ ἢ δάκρυα,
κι ἀνάμεσα σὲ τόσα διφορούμενα:
βροχὴ ἢ δάκρυα,
ἔρωτας ἢ τρόπος νὰ μεγαλώνουμε,
ἐσὺ ἢ μικρὴ ἀποχαιρετιστήρια αἰώρηση σκιᾶς
τοῦ τελευταίου φύλλου.
Τὸ κάθε τελευταῖο,
τελευταῖο τ' ὀνομάζω χωρὶς ἐπιφύλαξη.

Καὶ μεγάλωσα πολὺ
γιὰ νὰ εἶναι αὐτὸ ἀφορμὴ δακρύων.
Δάκρυα ἢ βροχή, ποῦ νὰ ξέρω;
Καὶ μένω νὰ ἐξαρτιέμαι ἀπὸ σταγόνες.
Καὶ μεγάλωσα πολὺ
γιὰ νὰ περιμένω ἄλλο μέτρο ὅταν βρέχει
κι ὅταν δὲν βρέχει ἄλλο.
Σταγόνες γιὰ ὅλα.

THE DISJUNCTIVE *OR*

The rain has shut me in
and now I'm left depending on drops.

But how to know whether it's rain
or tears from a memory's inner sky?
I've grown too old to label
these phenomena without reservation,
this one rain, that one tears.

Dry, I stand between
the two possibilities: rain or tears,
and among all too many ambiguities:
rain or tears,
love or a way of growing old,
you or the little dangling farewell
of the last leaf's shadow.
I label every last
last without reservation.

And I've grown too old
to make this an occasion for tears.
Tears or rain, how to know?
And now I'm left depending on drops.
And I've grown too old
to expect one measure when it rains
and another when it doesn't.
Drops for everything.

Σταγόνες βροχῆς ἢ δάκρυα.

Ἀπὸ τὰ μάτια κάποιας μνήμης ἢ τὰ δικά μου.

Ἐγὼ ἢ μνήμη, ποῦ νὰ ξέρω;

Μεγάλωσα πολὺ γιὰ νὰ χωρίζω τοὺς χρόνους.

Βροχὴ ἢ δάκρυα.

Ἐσὺ ἢ μικρὴ ἀποχαιρετιστήρια αἰώρηση σκιᾶς
τοῦ τελευταίου φύλλου.

Raindrops or tears.

From some memory's eyes or from my own.

I or the memory, how to know?

I've grown too old to tell the times apart.

Rain or tears.

You or the little dangling farewell

of the last leaf's shadow.

ΤΥΧΗ ΚΟΙΝΗ

Οἱ δρόμοι μου,
οἱ δρόμοι σας
κι αὐτό.

Ἐκεῖνος,
ἐγὼ
κι αὐτό.

Οἱ νυμφίοι Μάιοι,
τὸ κατάλληλο ἔνδυμα
κι αὐτό.

Τὸ ἄμαχο αἴσθημα,
τὸ κρυμμένο μαχαίρι
κι αὐτό.

Ἡ ὁδεύουσα δίψα,
ἡ καλὴ Σαμαρεῖτις
κι αὐτό.

Ἡ μακροζωία τῶν ὀνείρων,
ἡ ἐργατικότης τῶν ἐλπίδων
κι αὐτό.

Οἱ ἄλτες ὅρκοι πάνω ἀπὸ τὸ χρόνο,
ἡ φυλλοβόλος μνήμη
κι αὐτό.

•

COMMON FATE

My roads,
your roads
and this.

He,
I
and this.

The bridegroom Mays,
the appropriate attire
and this.

The noncombatant feeling,
the hidden knife
and this.

The advancing thirst,
the Samaritan woman
and this.

The longevity of dreams,
the assiduousness of hopes
and this.

Oaths vaulting over time,
the deciduous memory
and this.

•

Ὁ ἀπαραίτητος ἥλιος,
ἡ ξαφνικὴ ὡραία διάθεση
κι αὐτό.

Ἡ ἅμιλλα τῶν κίτρινων φύλλων
γιὰ μιὰ ψύχραιμη πτώση,
ἡ ποίηση ποὺ τὰ ἐμψυχώνει
κι αὐτό.

Ἡ ἀνομβρία,
ἡ βροχὴ
κι αὐτό.

Ἡ ἀγωνία σας,
ἡ ἀγωνία μου
κι αὐτό.

Ἡ μύηση τῶν ἀγαλμάτων
στὶς δικές μας μεθόδους ἀνίας,
ἡ θυσία ὅλο καὶ κάποιας Ἰφιγένειας
γιὰ ἕνα ψωροφύσημα ἀνέμου
κι αὐτό.

Ἡ ἐκγύμναση τῶν λέξεων
νὰ περνοῦν μέσ' ἀπ' τὴ σιωπή,
ἡ ἐκγύμναση τῆς σιωπῆς
νὰ περνᾶ μέσ' ἀπ' τὶς λέξεις
κι αὐτό.

•

The necessary sun,
the sudden good mood
and this.

The yellow leaves' contending
to fall valiantly,
the song that steels their souls
and this.

The drought,
the rain
and this.

Your anguish,
my anguish
and this.

The statues' initiation
into our own rituals of boredom,
the sacrifice of yet another Iphigenia
to one more third-rate gust of wind
and this.

The training of words
to pass through silence,
the training of silence
to pass through words
and this.

•

Τὸ αὐστηρῶς φρουρούμενο μέλλον
κι ἡ ἁρπαγή του στὸ τέλος
ἀπ᾽ αὐτό:

Τὸ ἀνώφελο.

The strictly guarded future
and its final abduction
by this:

Pointlessness.

Η ΠΕΡΙΦΡΑΣΤΙΚΗ ΠΕΤΡΑ

Μίλα.
Πὲς κάτι, ὁτιδήποτε.
Μόνο μὴ στέκεις σὰν ἀτσάλινη ἀπουσία.
Διάλεξε ἔστω κάποια λέξη,
ποὺ νὰ σὲ δένει πιὸ σφιχτὰ
μὲ τὴν ἀοριστία.
Πές:
«ἄδικα»,
«δέντρο»,
«γυμνό».
Πές:
«θὰ δοῦμε»,
«ἀστάθμητο»,
«βάρος».
Ὑπάρχουν τόσες λέξεις ποὺ ὀνειρεύονται
μιὰ σύντομη, ἄδετη, ζωὴ μὲ τὴ φωνή σου.

Μίλα.
Ἔχουμε τόση θάλασσα μπροστά μας.
Ἐκεῖ ποὺ τελειώνουμε ἐμεῖς
ἀρχίζει ἡ θάλασσα.
Πὲς κάτι.
Πὲς «κύμα», ποὺ δὲν στέκεται.
Πὲς «βάρκα», ποὺ βουλιάζει
ἂν τὴν παραφορτώσεις μὲ προθέσεις.
Πὲς «στιγμή»,

THE PERIPHRASTIC STONE

Speak.

Say something, anything.

Don't just stand there like a steel absence.

Choose just one word

that will bind you tighter

to indecisiveness.

Say:

"unjustly,"

"tree,"

"naked."

Say:

"we'll see,"

"imponderable,"

"weight."

There are so many words that dream

of a brief, unbound life beside your voice.

Speak.

There is so much sea before us.

Where we end

the sea begins.

Say something.

Say "wave," which won't stand still.

Say "rowboat," which sinks

if overloaded with intentions.

Say "instant,"

ποὺ φωνάζει βοήθεια ὅτι πνίγεται,
μὴν τὴ σώζεις,
πὲς
«δὲν ἄκουσα».

Μίλα.
Οἱ λέξεις ἔχουν ἔχθρες μεταξύ τους,
ἔχουν τοὺς ἀνταγωνισμούς:
ἂν κάποια ἀπ᾿ αὐτὲς σ᾿ αἰχμαλωτίσει,
σ᾿ ἐλευθερώνει ἄλλη.
Τράβα μιὰ λέξη ἀπ᾿ τὴ νύχτα
στὴν τύχη.
Ὁλόκληρη νύχτα στὴν τύχη.
Μὴ λὲς «ὁλόκληρη»,
πὲς «ἐλάχιστη»,
ποὺ σ᾿ ἀφήνει νὰ φύγεις.
Ἐλάχιστη
αἴσθηση,
λύπη
ὁλόκληρη
δική μου.
Ὁλόκληρη νύχτα.

Μίλα.
Πὲς «ἀστέρι», ποὺ σβήνει.
Δὲν λιγοστεύει ἡ σιωπὴ μὲ μιὰ λέξη.
Πὲς «πέτρα»,
ποὺ εἶναι ἄσπαστη λέξη.

which shouts *help*, it's drowning,
don't save it,
say
"didn't hear a thing."

Speak.
Words hold grudges,
engage in rivalries:
if one of them holds you captive,
another sets you free.
Draw a word out of the night
at random.
An entire night at random.
Don't say "entire,"
say "tiny,"
which releases you.
Tiny
sensation,
entire
sadness
all mine.
An entire night.

Speak.
Say "star," which vanishes.
Silence is not diminished by one word.
Say "stone,"
an unbreakable word.

Ἔτσι, ἴσα ἴσα,
νὰ βάλω ἕναν τίτλο
σ' αὐτὴ τὴ βόλτα τὴν παραθαλάσσια.

So, barely so
I can put a title
on this walk along the seashore.

ΜΑΥΡΗ ΓΡΑΒΑΤΑ

Πότιζε σὺ τὴ γλάστρα
κι ἄσε νὰ κλαίω.
Μόνο γράφε τοὺς λόγους,
μήπως κι ὀφείλω κι ἄλλη λύπη.
Θέλω νὰ ἔχω τὴ συνείδησή μου ἥσυχη
πὼς βασανίστηκα γιὰ ὅλα.

Γράψε πὼς κλαίω γιὰ ἕναν καθρέφτη.
Ἄλλοτε διακοσμητικὸ στοιχεῖο,
μαντεῖο τώρα.
Γιὰ τὴν ξερὴ *καληνύχτα*
ποὺ λὲν οἱ μικρὲς πιθανότητες
καὶ ξοφλᾶνε.
Γράψε πὼς κλαίω γιὰ τὸ παράθυρό σου,
κλειστὸ κι ἀκαλημέριστο
καὶ μελαγχολικὸ ἐκ γενετῆς του.
Γιὰ τὰ πουλιὰ τῆς τελευταίας δεκαετίας.
Τὸν τρόμο τους μὲ τὶς κεραῖες τηλεοψίας.
Γιὰ τὴν προσαρμογή τους ὕστερα,
καὶ τὰ πετάγματά τους
σ' αὐτὰ τὰ σιδερένια δέντρα.
Ποὺ μάθανε νὰ τραγουδοῦν
σὲ σιδερένιους κλώνους.

Γράφε.
Γι' αὐτὸ τὸ Σαββατόβραδο ποὺ θάφτηκε
ἀνάμεσα σὲ δύο κυπαρίσσια

BLACK TIE

Just water the plant
and let me weep.
But write down the reasons,
in case I owe some more sorrow.
I want to settle my conscience
that I have suffered for everything.

Write that I weep over a mirror.
Once a decorative object,
now an oracle.
Over the terse *goodnight*
uttered by the slightest chances
before they clear out.
Write that I weep over your window,
shut and unsaluted
and melancholy from birth.
Over the birds of the past decade.
Their dread of television antennas.
Over their adjustment later
and their flights
through these iron trees.
Over their learning to sing
on iron branches.

Write.
About this Saturday night, buried
between two cypresses

στὴ Φραγκόκλησα.
Γιὰ τὸ φεγγάρι ποὺ πενθεῖ — φοράει
μαύρη γραβάτα σύννεφο,
γράψε πὼς κλαίει.
Κλαίω γιατὶ μὲ ρώτησες
ἂν εἶδα τὴν πανσέληνο.
Ὄχι, δὲν εἶδα τίποτα γεμάτο καὶ δὲν ἔζησα.
Κλαίω ποὺ τὰ παιδιὰ κρατοῦν τὴ σάκα τους
σὰν τελειωμένη κιόλας γνώση,
καὶ στῶν ἀγίνωτων ὡρῶν
τὴν τρυφερὴ καθησύχασι δὲν πᾶνε
καὶ δὲν παίζουν.

Γράψε πὼς κλαίω γιὰ τὶς μητέρες.
Τὶς πιὸ παλιὲς μητέρες μου.
Τὶς λεπτὲς κι ὄμορφες,
τῶν παραθύρων ἐρωμένες,
ἁρπίστριες τοῦ ἀγναντέματος,
ποὺ τὶς ἐπῆρε ἀπρόφταστες ὁ θάνατος
κι αὐτὲς μακροημερεύουν μητρικὲς
σὲ σαλονιοῦ φωτογραφίες
καὶ σὲ κεντήματα.

Κλαίω γιατὶ ἀνάψανε τὰ φῶτα
κι ἡ Κυριακὴ κουλουριασμένη γάτα
στὸ παράθυρό μου.
Ὁ φόβος βάζει τὰ καλά του
καὶ περιμένει.

•

outside the French church.
About the moon in mourning—
in a black-tie cloud—
write that *it* weeps.
I weep because you asked me
if I saw the full moon.
No, I've seen nothing full, nor have I lived fully.
I weep because children carry their schoolbags
like knowledge already obsolete
and in the soothing playground
of their unripe hours they do not go
and do not play.

Write that I weep over the mothers.
My oldest mothers.
The slim and fair ones
the window-lovers,
who play the harp of distance with their eyes,
whom death took unprepared,
who last through long maternal lives
in drawing-room photographs
and embroideries.

I weep because lights are lit
and Sunday is a cat
curled up in my window.
Fear is all dressed up
and waits.

•

Γράφε.
Πὼς κλαίω γιὰ τοὺς τυφῶνες,
τὸ λίγο φαΐ,
τὸ κάθε Λίγο,
γιὰ τοὺς σεισμοὺς
χωρὶς προειδοποίηση.
Κλαίω ἐπειδὴ χαμένη πάει
ἡ εἴδηση ποὺ μοῦ 'φερες
πὼς εἶδες χθὲς τὴν πρώτη πεταλούδα.
Κλαίω γιατὶ δὲν εἶναι εἴδηση τὸ ἐφήμερο.

Γράφε. Κλαίω
ἐπειδὴ ἡ τύχη κλείστηκε στὸ σπίτι της,
ἡ ἀναβολὴ ἔφτασε στὸν δήμιο,
τὸ παγούρι ἔχει φτάσει στὴν ἔρημο,
ἡ νεότης ἔχει φτάσει στὴ φωτογραφία.
Κλαίω γιατὶ ποιὸς ξέρει ποιὸς θὰ κλείσει
τῶν ἡμερῶν μου τὰ μάτια.

Πότιζε σὺ τὴ γλάστρα
κι ἄσε νὰ κλαίω ἐπειδή...

Write.
That I weep about typhoons,
too little food,
every Too Little,
about earthquakes
that come without warning.
I weep because the news you brought me—
that yesterday you saw the first butterfly—
is of no use.
I weep because the ephemeral is no news.

Write. I weep
because luck shut itself up in the house,
the deferment reached the hangman,
the flask reached the desert,
youth reached the photograph.
I weep because who knows who will close
the eyes of my days.

Just water the plant
and let me weep because . . .

ΤΟ ΤΕΛΕΥΤΑΙΟ ΣΩΜΑ ΜΟΥ (1981)

MY LAST BODY (1981)

ΤΟ ΤΕΛΕΥΤΑΙΟ ΣΩΜΑ ΜΟΥ

Σ' ἐσένα, Αἴφνης, ἀπευθύνομαι.

Αἴφνης ὀνειροδίαιτο,
τρελὰ γενναῖο, καλλονό,
νόθο παιδὶ ἀγνώστων παραγόντων,
σ' ἐσένα ποὺ τὸ Σπάνιο
Σπάνιο τὸ διατηρεῖς,
δείχνοντας γρανιτώδη ἀδιαφορία
στὸ ὀδυνηρό, τὸ λάγνο πάθος
ποὺ τρέφει γιὰ σένα ἡ Συχνότητα.
Σπίθα ἀπ' τὴν ἐπίμονη τριβὴ
μιᾶς προσμονῆς καὶ μιᾶς παραίτησης,
ποὺ στάμνες καὶ δίψες γεμίζεις
χωρὶς τὴ σύμπραξη κρήνης, πηγῆς.
Χρόνε Θεοκατέβατε,
μικρόσωμε,
ποὺ τὴν τεράστια δύναμή σου συσσωρεύεις
ἀργοπορία συσσωρεύοντας,
Μεσσία μονολεκτικέ,
σεισμὲ ποὺ γκρεμίζεις
τὰ ἀντισεισμικά μας Ἀμετάβλητα,
σ' ἐσένα Αἴφνης, κοσμοφόρα Μεσολάβηση,
σπαρακτικὰ ἀπευθύνομαι
νὰ 'ρθεῖς νὰ ἐλευθερώσεις
τὸ τελευταῖο σῶμα μου ἐδῶ πάνω
τὸν δουλοπάροικο παλμό του
νὰ ἐλευθερώσεις

MY LAST BODY

To you, *Suddenly,* I appeal.

Dreamfed *Suddenly,*
insanely brave, beautiful,
bastard of unknown factors,
to you who keep what's Rare
Rare,
displaying a granite indifference
to the sad, wanton passion
Recurrence feels for you.
To you, a spark from the steady friction
between expectation and renunciation,
to you who fills jugs and thirsts
unaided by any fountain or source.
To you, Godfallen
small-bodied Time,
who amasses huge power
and thus amasses delay,
one-word Messiah,
seismic shock that brings down
our anti-seismic Invariables,
to you, *Suddenly,* world-bearing Mediation,
sorely I appeal:
Come up here and liberate
my last body,
liberate
its slave heartbeat

ἀπὸ τὸν πιὸ σκληρὸ

τὸν πιὸ αἱμόφιλο

τὸν παρανοϊκὸ ποὺ μοῦ 'τυχε ἀφέντη

τὸν *σήκω-κάτσε*

σήκω-κάτσε

σήκω-κάτσε...

from the bloodiest
cruelest
paranoid master I ever had, the
Go up and do the attic
go down and do the cellar
you can do them both together . . .

ΤΟ ΠΛΗΣΙΕΣΤΕΡΟ

Κάτι πρωτόβγαλτα ὡς φαίνεται
στὸν κόσμο καὶ τοὺς νόμους του πουλάκια
κι ἐντούτοις ἤδη κουρασμένα
γιατὶ δὲν εἶναι τὰ φτερὰ
ἄπτωτη εὔνοια καὶ προνόμιο,
ρωτοῦν ἐμένα, ποιόν, ἐμένα,
ποῦ εἶν' τὸ πλησιέστερο κλαδὶ
γιὰ ν' ἀκουμπήσουν.
Δὲν εἴμαστε καλά. Ἂν ἤξερα ἐγὼ
ποῦ εἶν' τὸ Πλησιέστερο
ὅτι ἔχει καὶ βαθμὸ συγκριτικὸ
τὸ ἀνύπαρκτο Πλησίον,
θά 'τρεχα νὰ τὸ πιάσω πρώτη ἐγώ,
ὅλο κι ἀπαραχώρητο,
κι ἂς ψόφαγαν πουλάκια
δίκια καὶ προτεραιότητες
— κλαδιὰ σπασμένα τὸ ἀλληλέγγυο.

Ἂς πᾶνε τὰ πουλάκια
τὴ μεγάλη Πεῖρα νὰ ρωτήσουν
ν' ἀκούσουν ὅ,τι εἶπε καὶ σ' ἐμένα
ὅταν ξεθεωμένη ἀπὸ κούραση ἄφτερη
τὴ ρώτησα ποῦ εἶναι ν' ἀκουμπήσω
τὸ πλησιέστερο κλαδί.
Δὲν εἴμαστε καλὰ εἶχε καγχάσει
ἡ μεγάλη Πεῖρα: ἂν ἤξερα ἐγὼ
ποῦ εἶν' τὸ Πλησιέστερο
θά 'τρεχα νὰ τὸ πιάσω πρώτη,

NEAREST

Some little birds, seemingly unversed
in the world and its laws,
but nonetheless already tired —
since wings are not
an infallible favor or privilege —
ask me, of all people,
where is the nearest branch
for them to rest on.
They must be kidding. If I knew
where Nearest was,
or that a superlative exists
for a nonexistent Near
I'd rush to occupy it first myself,
all of it, inalienable,
too bad if little birds die
along with rights and priorities
— solidarity is nothing but broken branches.
Let the little birds go
ask great Experience
and listen to what she told me too
when, wingless and dead tired,
I asked her where the nearest branch
for me to rest on is.
You must be kidding, great Experience
chuckled: if I knew
where Nearest was
I'd rush to occupy it first myself,

ὅλο κι ἀπαραχώρητο,
κι ἂς ψόφαγες ἐσὺ
γιατὶ τὸ πλησιέστερο κλαδὶ
εἶναι ὁ θάνατός σου ἡ ζωή μου.

all of it inalienable,
too bad if you should die,
because the nearest branch
means *your death for my life.*

Ο ΠΡΟ-ΔΗΜΙΟΣ

Ὅμοια μ᾽ Ἐκεῖνο καθὼς οἱ δίδυμοι.

Ὅμως αὐτὴν φοβᾶμαι πιὸ πολὺ
γιατὶ ἔρχεται πιὸ γρήγορα ἀπὸ Ἐκεῖνο,
τρέχει κι ἔρχεται μαρτυριάρα του
ἐνῶ σὰν μυστικὸ ἀμέριμνο βαδίζει ἀκόμα Ἐκεῖνο.
Δὲν τὴ βλέπεις
ἀλλὰ περνάει τὸ τρέξιμό της
σιφουνικὸ ἀπὸ μέσα σου,
κλυδωνισμός,
δὲν πέφτεις μὰ γκρεμίζεσαι,
καπνοὶ σὲ ζώνουν πυρκαγιᾶς
ἐνῶ χλωρὸ ἀκόμα εἶναι τὸ δάσος
καὶ τὸ νερὸ ποὺ ἔχεις μαζέψει
σὲ στάμνες καὶ παρασταμνάκια
πιωμένο πρὶν τὸ πιεῖς.
Ἔρχεται μαρτυριάρα του πιὸ γρήγορα
ὄχι νὰ σώσει νὰ περισώσει
οὔτε καὶ νὰ προετοιμάσει,
γιατὶ κανεὶς ποτὲ
ἂν καὶ καλὰ προετοιμασμένος
προετοιμασμένος δὲν βρέθηκε
δὲν βρέθηκε ἕτοιμος νὰ χάσει.
Μὲ τὸν πιὸ γρήγορο ἐρχομό της
σαδιστικὰ προσυμβαίνει
αὐτὸ ποὺ εἶναι νὰ συμβεῖ.
Λὲς καὶ δὲν χάνεις γευστικὰ
χάνοντας μιὰ φορὰ αὐτὸ ποὺ χάνεις,

THE PRE-HANGMAN

Identical to That, just like twins.
I, however, am far more afraid of This
because This gets there quicker than That,
comes running like a tattletale on That,
while That still walks around like a carefree secret.
You don't see it
but its tornado course
sweeps through you,
pitching and rolling,
you don't fall straight down, you tumble,
surrounded by smoke from a huge fire,
while the forest remains green
and the water you collected
in pitchers large and small
has been drunk before you drink it.
This comes like a tattletale on That,
not to save, to salvage,
nor to prepare,
because nobody ever,
even if well-prepared,
was found well prepared,
was found ready to lose.
Because This comes more quickly
what is supposed to happen
sadistically pre-happens.
As if you do not lose the taste
by losing once what you lose,

πρέπει καὶ νὰ προ–χάνεις
ἀπὸ τὸ χέρι τοῦ προ–δήμιου
τῆς Προαίσθησης,
τῆς μαρτυριάρας τοῦ Ἐπερχόμενου.

you must also pre-lose
at the pre-hangman's hands,
Premonition
—the tattletale of What's-to-Come.

ΧΡΟΝΙΚΟ ΚΑΡΠΩΝ ΚΑΙ ΑΚΑΡΠΩΝ

Στὴ Σπάρτη,
τὰ πορτοκάλια πάνω ποὺ φεῦγαν ἀπ' τὸ ἄγουρο.
Γιὰ νὰ γλυκάνουν.
Τὴ μεταβατικὴ ἀπόφασή τους
συνόδευε ὣς πιὸ κάτω
τὸ πρὶν χρῶμα,
ποὺ σὰν νὰ τὴ φοβόταν τὴ βιάση πρὸς τὸ ὥριμο
κι ὅλο κοντοστεκόταν
βαθὺ δύσπιστο πράσινο.
Τὸ πηγαινέλα τοῦ χυμοῦ
στὸν ἐπαμφοτερίζοντα καρπό,
στὴν ἔτσι κι ἔτσι φλούδα,
ζητοῦσε μιὰ ἀπευκταία ὁλοκλήρωση.

Ὄχι μόνο στὰ πορτοκάλια.
Κάποια παρεμφερὴς διεργασία καὶ σ' ἐμένα.
Κάτι ἐλευθερωνότανε τρομάζοντας.
Μιὰ ἀγωνία ὡρίμαζε καὶ σάπιζε σὲ κόπο.
Γιὰ νὰ γλυκάνω.
Τὸ πηγαινέλα τοῦ πικροῦ
στὴν ἐπαμφοτερίζουσα πληγή,
στὴν ἔτσι κι ἔτσι μοίρα,
ζητοῦσε ἕνα φτάνει πιά.

Στὸν Μυστρᾶ,
λαχάνιασμα τῆς Ἱστορίας,

CHRONICLE OF THE FRUIT AND THE UNFRUITFUL

In Sparta,
oranges were just leaving unripeness.
So they would sweeten.
Their transitional decision
was accompanied on the way
by their former color,
which seemed to fear the rush toward ripening
and kept lingering,
in deep mistrustful green.
The coming and going of the juice
in the irresolute fruit
in this undecided peel
sought an undesired completion.

Not only in the oranges.
Some similar process also inside me.
Something in there shook loose and got scared.
Anxiety was ripening and rotting into weariness.
So I would sweeten.
The coming and going of bitterness
in the irresolute wound,
in the undecided fate,
called for *enough is enough.*

In Mystras,
a gasping of History,

ἀποθέωσι τῆς πέτρας.

Ἐρείπια

καὶ ἐρείπια τοῦ ἀνατρέχω.

Τὰ σκαλοπάτια ὡς ἀπάνω

καὶ τὰ ὄχι σκαλοπάτια ὡς ἀπάνω.

Ἀναποδογυρισμένοι θρόνοι

καὶ χρόνοι μαρμάρινοι,

καμάρες καὶ θόλοι,

ρόλοι ἐκθρονισμένοι.

Γιὰ νὰ γλυκάνω.

Νὰ βγῶ ἀπὸ τὰ χαλάσματα,

τὸ χαλασμό,

ἀπὸ τὰ χαλασμένα ὅλα

μ' ἕνα τραγούδι.

Μὰ τὰ τραγούδια

εἶναι γυαλιὰ σπασμένα ὅπου πατήσεις,

βιογραφίες τῶν νερῶν ποὺ ἤπιες

καὶ δὲν ἤπιες,

τὸ χαρακίρι μὲ ὀνόματα καὶ λεπτοδεῖκτες

ποὺ ἔκανες.

Ρόλοι ἐκθρονισμένοι.

Στὴν ἐκκλησία τῆς Περιβλέπτου

τὸ Πολυχρόνιο τοῦ Τότε.

Αὐτοκράτορες ἴσκιοι.

Ἔκανα πὼς δὲν εἶδα τοὺς Παλαιολόγους

κι οὔτε ταράχτηκα

an apotheosis of stones.
Ruins
and the ruins of remembering.
The steps to the top
and the non-steps to the top.
Toppled thrones
and ages in marble
arches and vaults
dethroned roles.

So I would sweeten.
And get away from the destruction,
the destroying,
all that's been destroyed,
with a song.
Songs, however,
are splintered glass wherever you set foot,
life histories of every water you've drunk
or haven't
every hara-kiri you committed
with names and minute hands

Dethroned roles.
In the Peribleptos Church
a Polychronion for Then.
Emperors' shadows.
I pretended not to see the Palaiologos
nor was I upset

ποὺ τὸν δικό σου θρόνο καλόβλεπε μιὰν ἀράχνη.

Κι ἄναψα ἕνα κερὶ στοὺς Ἅγιους Λόγους
κάθε Πτώσης.

when I noticed your throne coveted by a spider.
And I lit a candle to the Divine Logos
of every fall.

ΧΑΙΡΕ ΠΟΤΕ' (1988)

HAIL NEVER (1988)

ΑΠΡΟΣΔΟΚΙΕΣ

Θεέ μου τί δὲν μᾶς περιμένει ἀκόμα.

Κάθομαι ἐδῶ καὶ κάθομαι.
Βρέχει χωρὶς νὰ βρέχει
ὅπως ὅταν σκιὰ
μᾶς ἐπιστρέφει σῶμα.

Κάθομαι ἐδῶ καὶ κάθομαι.
Ἐγὼ ἐδῶ, ἀπέναντι ἡ καρδιά μου
καὶ πιὸ μακριὰ
ἡ κουρασμένη σχέση μου μαζί της.
Ἔτσι, γιὰ νὰ φαινόμαστε πολλοὶ
κάθε ποὺ μᾶς μετράει τὸ ἄδειο.

Φυσάει ἄδειο δωμάτιο.
Πιάνομαι γερὰ ἀπὸ τὸν τρόπο μου
ποὺ ἔχω νὰ σαρώνομαι.

Νέα σου δὲν ἔχω.
Ἡ φωτογραφία σου στάσιμη.
Κοιτάζεις σὰν ἐρχόμενος
χαμογελᾶς σὰν ὄχι.
Ἄνθη ἀποξηραμένα στὸ πλάι
σοῦ ἐπαναλαμβάνουν ἀσταμάτητα
τὸ ἄκρατο ὄνομά τους semprevives
semprevives — αἰώνιες, αἰώνιες
μὴν τύχει καὶ ξεχάσεις τί δὲν εἶσαι.

•

NONEXPECTATIONS

My God, what is *not* to come.

I sit here and sit.
It rains without raining
as when a shadow
returns a body to us.

I sit here and sit.
I here, my heart opposite
and still more distant
my tired relationship with it.
Just so, to give the impression we are many
every time the emptiness takes attendance.

An empty room is blowing.
I firmly hang on to how
I get swept away.

No news from you.
Your photograph stationary.
You look as if you're on your way
you smile as if you're not.
Dried flowers to one side
ceaselessly repeat
their unsoiled name *sempervivum*
sempervivum — everlasting, everlasting
so you won't forget what you are not.

·

Μὲ ρωτάει ὁ καιρὸς
ἀπὸ ποῦ θέλω νὰ περάσει
ποῦ ἀκριβῶς τονίζομαι
στὸ γέρνω ἢ στὸ γερνῶ.
Ἀστειότητες.
Κανένα τέλος δὲν γνωρίζει ὀρθογραφία.

Νέα σου δὲν ἔχω.
Ἡ φωτογραφία σου στάσιμη.
Ὅπως βρέχει χωρὶς νὰ βρέχει.

Ὅπως σκιὰ μοῦ ἐπιστρέφει σῶμα.
Κι ὅπως θὰ συναντηθοῦμε μιὰ μέρα
ἐκεῖ πάνω.
Σὲ κάποιαν ἀραιότητα κατάφυτη
μὲ σκιερὲς ἀπροσδοκίες
καὶ ἀειθαλεῖς περιστροφές.
Τὸν διερμηνέα τῆς σφοδρῆς
σιωπῆς ποὺ θὰ αἰσθανθοῦμε
—μορφὴ ἐξελιγμένη τῆς σφοδρῆς
μέθης ποὺ προκαλεῖ μία συνάντηση
ἐδῶ κάτω— θὰ 'ρθεῖ νὰ κάνει ἕνα κενό.
Καὶ θὰ μᾶς συνεπάρει τότε
μιὰ ἀγνωρισιὰ παράφορη
— μορφὴ ἐξελιγμένη τοῦ ἀγκαλιάσματος
ποὺ ἐφαρμόζει ἡ συνάντηση ἐδῶ κάτω.
Ναὶ θὰ συναντηθοῦμε. Εὐανάπνευστα, κρυφὰ
ἀπὸ τὴν ἕλξη. Κάτω ἀπὸ δυνατὴ βροχὴ

Time asks me
where I want it to pass
whether I see myself as
bending or ending.
Witticisms.
No end knows anything about wordplay.

No news from you.
Your photograph stationary.
As it rains without raining.

As a shadow returns a body to me.
And as we will meet up there
one day.
In some barrens overgrown
with shady nonexpectations
and evergreen circumlocutions.
The interpreter of the acute
silence we will feel
—a refined form of acute
elation an encounter down here
induces—will be a void.
Then we will be enraptured
by a passionate nonrecognition
—a refined form of embrace
encounters practice down here.
Yes we will meet. Breathing freely, behind
attraction's back. Under the heavy downpour

ραγδαίας ἔλλειψης βαρύτητας. Σὲ κάποιαν
ἴσως ἐκδρομὴ τοῦ ἀπείρου στὸ ἐπ' ἄπειρον·
στὴν τελετὴ ἀπονομῆς ἀπωλειῶν στὸ γνωστό,
γιὰ τὴ μεγάλη προσφορά του στὸ ἄγνωστο·
καλεσμένοι σὲ ἀστροφεγγιὰ προορισμοῦ,
σὲ διασκεδάσεις παύσεων γιὰ φιλευδιάλυτους
σκοποὺς καὶ ἀποχαιρετιστήριες οὐρανῶν
πρώην μεγάλες σημασίες.
Μόνο ποὺ ἐτούτη ἡ συντροφιὰ τῶν ἀποστάσεων
θὰ εἶναι κάπως ἄκεφη, ἀνεύθυμη
κι ἂς εὐθυμεῖ ἐκ τοῦ μηδενὸς ἡ ἀνυπαρξία.
Ἴσως γιατὶ θὰ λείπει ἡ ψυχὴ τῆς παρέας.
                                                            Ἡ σάρκα.
Φωνάζω τὴ στάχτη
νὰ μὲ ξαρματώσει.
Καλῶ τὴ στάχτη
μὲ τὸ συνθηματικό της ὄνομα: Ὅλα.

Θὰ συναντιέστε ὑποθέτω τακτικὰ
ἐσὺ κι ὁ θάνατος ἐκείνου τοῦ ὀνείρου.
Τὸ στερνοπαίδι ὄνειρο.

Ἀπ' ὅσα εἶχα τὸ πιὸ φρόνιμο.
Ξεθολωμένο, πρᾶο, συνεννοητικό.
Ὄχι καὶ τόσο βέβαια ὀνειροπόλο
ἀλλὰ οὔτε καὶ φτηνὰ χαμηλωμένο,
ὄχι σουδάριο κάθε γῆς.
Πολὺ οἰκονόμο ὄνειρο,

of a fierce lack of gravity. Maybe during
an excursion of infinity to the infinite;
at the ceremony where the Known is awarded with losses
for its great contribution to the Unknown;
guests at destiny's starlight,
at cessations' galas for soluble
causes and at farewell parties for the skies'
formerly great significances.
It's just that this gathering of distances
will be a bit morose, ill-tempered
even if nonexistence is good-tempered for nothing.
Perhaps because the soul of the party will be missing.

The flesh.

I ask the ashes
to disarm me.
I call the ashes
by their code name: All.

I suppose you meet regularly
you and that dream's death.
The last-born dream.

The wisest I ever had.
Lucid, kind, conciliatory.
Not very dreamy of course
not brought down dirt cheap either,
not a shroud for every earth.
A dream very thrifty

σὲ ἔνταση καὶ λάθη.
Ἀπὸ τὰ ὄνειρα ποὺ ἀνάθρεψα
τὸ πιὸ πονετικό μου: νὰ μὴ
γερνάω μόνη.

Θὰ συναντιέστε ὑποθέτω τακτικὰ
ἐσὺ κι ὁ θάνατός του.
Δίνε του χαιρετίσματα, πές του νὰ ᾿ρθεῖ
κι αὐτὸ μαζὶ ἐξάπαντος ὅταν συναντηθοῦμε
ἐκεῖ, στὴν τελετὴ ἀπονομῆς ἀπωλειῶν.

Ὅσο δὲ ζεῖς νὰ μ᾿ ἀγαπᾶς.
Ναὶ ναὶ μοῦ φτάνει τὸ ἀδύνατον.
Κι ἄλλοτε ἀγαπήθηκα ἀπ᾿ αὐτό.
Ὅσο δὲ ζεῖς νὰ μ᾿ ἀγαπᾶς.
Διότι νέα σου δὲν ἔχω.
Καὶ ἀλίμονο ἂν δὲ δώσει
σημεῖα ζωῆς τὸ παράλογο.

with both intensity and errors.
Of all the dreams I've raised
my most compassionate: not to
grow old alone.

I suppose you meet regularly
you and that dream's death.
Give it my regards, ask it to come
without fail when we meet
there, at the losses awards ceremony.

Love me as long as you do not live.
Yes, yes the impossible is enough for me.
I've been loved by it before.
Love me as long as you do not live.
Because I have no news from you.
And what a disaster it would be if the irrational
gave no sign of life.

Η ΓΛΥΚΥΤΑΤΗ ΑΒΕΒΑΙΟΤΗΣ

Τρισάγια κάθε τόσο
γιὰ νὰ δοθεῖ ἡ ὑπηκοότητα νεκροῦ
στὸν *κεκοιμημένον δοῦλον σου.*

Ὕψιστε, τί ἐννοεῖς
ἄλλο νεκρὸς καὶ ἄλλο δοῦλος.
Κι ἀπὸ πότε ἐπιτρέπεται
νὰ κοιμοῦνται ἔτσι βαθιὰ
ἀτιμώρητοι οἱ δοῦλοι.

Τὸν κεκοιμημένον δοῦλον σου.
Θέ μου, ἂν ἀπελευθερώνει ὁ θάνατος
ὅπως μᾶς τὸ ὑπόσχεται παρήγορη
ἡ γλυκυτάτη ἀβεβαιότης, ἐσὺ
γιατί τὸν θὲς ντὲ καὶ καλὰ δουλέμπορο;

Τὸν κεκοιμημένον.
Περὶ ὕπνου πρόκειται, Κύριε;
Μὰ τοῦ κολλάει ὕπνος τοῦ νεκροῦ
ἔτσι εὔκολα νυστάζει ἡ ἀπώλεια τῆς ζωῆς;
Ἐδῶ ἐμεῖς, δοῦλοι τοῦ ἀπάνω κόσμου ἀκόμα
κι ὅμως ποιὸς κλείνει μάτι
ἂν δὲν τὸν νανουρίσει ὅπως ξέρει
μόνο ἡ γιαγιά του ἡ βεβαιότης
μὲ τὴ γλυκιά της ρόδινη ἀφύπνιση.

•

SWEETEST UNCERTAINTY

Frequent prayers for the dead
so that citizenship may be granted
to *thy servant who has fallen asleep.*

Almighty God, what do you mean by
dead is one thing and servant is another.
Since when are servants permitted
to sleep so deeply
and remain unpunished.

Thy servant who has fallen asleep.
If Death sets us free, dear God,
as sweetest Uncertainty
consolingly promises,
why insist he be our master?

Who has fallen asleep.
Is this about sleep, Lord?
Does sleep cleave to the dead,
can loss of life so easily doze off?
Still servants in the upper world, even we
cannot sleep a wink
without grandmother Certainty
lulling us — she alone knows how —
with her sweet rosy awakening.

•

Κύριε, μήπως ὅταν ἐνέκρινες
αὐτοὺς τοὺς ἀνελέπτους ἀνταγωνιστικοὺς ψαλμοὺς
ἤσουν ἀκόμη ἄνθρωπος;

Lord, could it be when you approved
these merciless contradictory psalms
you were still a man?

ΥΠΕΡ ΑΣΩΤΕΙΑΣ

Εἶμαι ἀνεβασμένη μὲ τὰ κιάλια μου
στὸ κατάρτι ἑνὸς ἀγκαθιοῦ ἐξασκοῦμαι
στοὺς φυσικοὺς πόνους τοὺς φέρνω πιὸ πλησίον.

Δειλινὰ λέγονται ἐκεῖνα τὰ χωνάκια
ποὺ γουρλώνουν τὰ φύλλα τους βραδάκι στὶς αὐλὲς
— τί μαζοχιστικὸ ὄνομα ποὺ διάλεξαν.

Ἀραιώνουν οἱ ἐκρήξεις τῶν κουκουναριῶν
προσέχει πιὰ ἡ ζέστη δὲν πετάει
σπίρτα ἀναμμένα.

Θεληματίας ἡ πρόνοια. Ἔζεψε τὰ μερμήγκια
ἀπὸ νωρὶς καὶ σπρῶξε σπρῶξε ἔχουν σύρει
ἀρκετὸ χειμώνα κιόλας στὴ φωλιά τους.

Ἀποταμίευση. Μιὰ σεβαστὴ ὁμολογῶ
μορφὴ χορτάτη εὐθανασίας.

Ἐν μέρει καλὰ τὰ λέει ὁ μύθος.
Ἔπρεπε νὰ λογικευτοῦν λίγο τὰ τζιτζίκια
νὰ βάζουν στὴν μπάντα μισὸ τραγούδι γιὰ τὸ κρύο
νὰ ἐξοικονομοῦν ὀλίγην
τῆς ὕπαρξής τους ἀσωτεία.

Ἔξω ἀπ' τὸ χορὸ καλὰ τὰ λέει ὁ μύθος.
Πῶς ἀλλιῶς νὰ κάνουν τὰ τζιτζίκια.

IN DEFENSE OF IMPROVIDENCE

Perched with my binoculars
on a thorn's mast, I'm training myself
in physical pain, I bring it closer.

Those little funnels are called moonflowers
evenings they open their leaves wide in gardens
—what a melancholy name they've chosen.

Pinecone explosions grow scarcer
heat now takes great care not to throw
lit matches.

Providence is a handyman. Early on it harnessed ants—
pushing and pulling they've already hauled
a good deal of winter into their nest.

Storing up. A respectable, I must admit, sated
form of euthanasia.

In part the fable is right.
The grasshoppers should be reasonable
set aside half a song for the cold
save some
of their life's improvidence.

Easy for the fable to say.
What else can grasshoppers do.

Δὲν ἀποταμιεύεται ἡ ἔνταση.
Δὲν θά 'θελε κι αὐτὴ νὰ ζεῖ περισσότερο;
Ὅμως δὲν ἀποταμιεύεται.
Μιὰ μέρα νὰ τὴ φυλάξεις χαλάει.

Κι εἶπα, ἔτσι ποὺ τὴ βλέπω
σωρηδὸν νὰ κεῖται ἄταφη ἄψαλτη
νὰ τῆς ῥίξω ἕνα ὁλάνθιστο Ἀμὴν
πρὶν τὴ διαμελίσει ἡ κατακραυγὴ
πρὶν τὴ σύρουν τροφὴ στὴ φωλιά τους
κάτι τομάρια ἑαυτούλικα μερμήγκια.

Intensity can't be stored.
Wouldn't it too want to live longer?
But it can't be stored.
Keep it just one day and it goes bad.

To see intensity like that, lying there
in a heap, unburied and unsung,
I thought of throwing a blossoming Amen on it
before the general outcry tears it to pieces
before some self-centered gimme-gimme ants
haul it off as food to their nest.

ΔΙΑΡΡΗΞΗ ΑΥΤΑΠΑΤΗΣ

Καὶ κάπου ἐν τῷ μέσῳ τῆς νυκτὸς
ἔλαμψε
ἕνα διανυκτερεῦον φαρμακεῖο.

Κύριε, δῶστε μου ἕνα ὑπνωτικὸ
νὰ κοιμηθεῖ λίγο ἡ ἔρημος ἔξω.

Κι ὡς νὰ ξεδιπλωθεῖ ἀπὸ τὴ νύστα του
ὁ φαρμακοποιός, θαύμαζα ἐγὼ
τὴν ἰσότητα τῶν πόνων στὰ ράφια
ἀνίατοι καὶ ἰάσιμοι, ὅλοι
σὲ ζωηρόχρωμα χαρούμενα κουτάκια.

Κι αἴφνης σὲ ἀναγνώρισα. Στὴν ἀπομόνωση.
Ψηλά· μόνο μάτι φόβου νὰ σὲ φτάνει.
Χαρογραφία σ' ἐτικέτα μπουκαλιοῦ μὲ δηλητήριο.

Ἀγνώριστη θανατηφόρα γεγυμνωμένη ἡ μορφή σου.
Τὰ χέρια σου φιγούρα φοβέρας χιαστὶ
ἐκεῖ στὴν ἀθώα θέση
ποὺ χάζευε ἄλλοτε ἀμέριμνα ὁ λαιμός σου.

Κύριε, ξεφώνισα
ταρακουνώντας τοὺς πόνους στὰ ράφια,
τί ἀποτρόπαια λάθη εἶν' αὐτὰ
πῶς χορηγεῖτε στοὺς νεκροὺς κι ἄλλο
παραπανίσιο δηλητήριο χωρὶς καινούργια

BREAKING INTO AN ILLUSION

And somewhere in the middle of the night
an all-night drugstore
shimmered.

Sir, give me a sleeping pill
so the desert out there gets some sleep.

And while the pharmacist
unfolded from his drowsiness, I admired
the equality of ailments on the shelves,
incurable and curable, all
in brightly colored, cheerful little boxes.

And suddenly I recognized you. In isolation.
Up there; where only fear's eye could catch you.
Charonography: a poison bottle's label.

Unrecognizable your lethal figure stripped bare.
Your hands formed a threat's crossed X
on that innocent spot
where your neck once nonchalantly dreamed.

Sir, I screamed,
while I shook the ailments on the shelves,
what horrid mistakes are these,
how can you administer to the dead
additional doses of poison with no new

συνταγὴ καὶ θέληση θεοῦ; Πῶς τολμᾶτε,
γιὰ νὰ διαφημίσετε δραστικὰ προϊόντα χάρου,
νὰ ξεκοκαλίζετε μορφὲς ποὺ ἐμεῖς δεινοπαθοῦμε
νὰ τὶς διατηρήσουμε δραστικὰ ὁλόκληρες
μέσα σὲ φιαλίδια σφραγισμένης αὐταπάτης;
Νὰ μοῦ ἐπιστρέψετε ἀμέσως τὸ πρωτότυπο.

Σᾶς πιστεύω, εἶπε ὁ φαρμακοποιός, ἀλλὰ
μετὰ τὴν ἀπομάκρυνσιν ἐκ τοῦ ταμείου
οὐδὲν λάθος ἀναγνωρίζεται.

prescription and no divine will? How dare you,
just to advertise drastic Charonic products,
rip the bones out of figures we've struggled hard
to keep drastically whole
in vials of sealed illusion?
Return the original to me immediately.

I understand, the pharmacist said, but
no error will be acknowledged
after leaving the counter.

ΧΑΙΡΕ ΠΟΤΕ'

Τελευταῖοι Χαιρετισμοὶ ἀπόψε
ἀτελείωτοι οἱ δικοί μου ποὺ σοῦ στέλνω
καὶ χαῖρε χαῖρε τοῦ ἀποκλείεται
ἡ θεία προθυμία νὰ σ' τοὺς δώσει.

Λιπόθυμα σωριάζονται βιολέτες
ἀπὸ τὸ σφιχταγκάλιασμα τοῦ χλιαροῦ
καιροῦ τὸ δικαιολογημένο
ἔχει ἀπὸ πέρσι νὰ τὶς δεῖ.

Χαῖρε συνέπεια λουλουδιῶν
πρὸς τὴν τακτὴν ἐπιστροφή σας
χαῖρε συνέπεια τοῦ ἀνεπίστρεπτου
τήρησες κατὰ γράμμα τοὺς νεκρούς.
Χαῖρε τοῦ σκοταδιοῦ τὸ σφιχταγκάλιασμα
ποὺ δέχεσαι τὸ δικαιολογημένο
ἔχει νὰ σὲ δεῖ πρὶν τὴ γέννησή σου.

Χαῖρε τῶν ματιῶν σου ἡ ἀνοιχτοφοβία
χαῖρε κεχαριτωμένη ὑπόσχεση τοῦ ἀνέλπιστου
πὼς βλέμμα σου θὰ ξεθαρρέψει πάλι κάποτε
νὰ ξανοιχτεῖ πρὸς ἔντρομο δικό μου.

Χαῖρε τῶν ματιῶν σου ἡ ἀνοιχτοφοβία
— τῆς μνήμης τὸ «ἐλευθέρας» νὰ πηγαίνει
ὅποτε θέλει νὰ τὰ βλέπει
αὐγὴ χαμένης μέρας.

Ὅσο γιὰ σένα κόσμε

HAIL NEVER

Tonight the Salutations came to an end
those I'm sending you are endless
and hail hail divine willingness's
refusal to convey them to you.

Violets fall into a swoon
from the mild weather's
embrace, understandably tight—
it hasn't seen them since last year.

Hail to you, flowers' constancy
in your regular return
hail no-return's constancy
respectful of the dead to the letter.
Hail darkness's embrace
that you welcome, understandably tight—
it hasn't seen you since before you were born.
Hail your eyes' fear of opening
hail the unhoped-for promise, full of grace,
that someday your gaze again may take courage
and open a path to my terrified gaze.
Hail your eyes' fear of opening
—memory's free pass for
a lost day's dawn
to go see them whenever it likes.

As for you, world,

ποὺ καταδέχεσαι νὰ ζεῖς
ὅσο ἔχει τὴν ἀνάγκη σου ἡ τύχη
γιὰ νὰ καρποῦνται τὰ δεινὰ
τὴν εὔφορη ἀντοχή σου,
ποὺ ἐξευτελίζεσαι νὰ ζεῖς
γιὰ νὰ σοῦ πεῖ μιὰ καλησπέρα τὸ πολὺ
κατὰ τὸν διάπλου
ἕνα ἐγγαστρίμυθα ὁλόγιομο φεγγάρι
τί νὰ σοῦ πῶ
χαῖρε κι ἐσύ.

condescending to live
as long as fortune needs you
so hardships reap the fruits
of your fertile endurance,
abasing yourself to live
so that a ventriloquist full moon
may bid you good evening
during transit
what more can I say
hail you too.

ΑΘΩΟ ΤΟ ΑΝΑΠΟΔΕΙΚΤΟ

Κύριε, γνωρίζω
σκαμμένους δρόμους ξανασκάβω
πρὶν ἀπὸ μένα ἔκυψαν βαθύτερα
πολλὲς ἐξερευνήτριες ἀγωνίες.
Ἀκλόνητη ἡ βασιλεία τοῦ ἀναπόδεικτου
(μεγάλος συκοφάντης σου μὰ καὶ ὑποστηρικτής σου).

Ψάχνω μήπως ἡ πίστη μας σ' ἐξώθησε νὰ γευτεῖς
τὸ χυμῶδες ἀξίωμα τοῦ Ὑπαίτιου
γιὰ ν' ἀποδυναμώσει κάπως τὸ Ἀνεξήγητο.

Ἐνεπλάκης ἢ ὄχι στῆς παντοδυναμίας τὸ ὀλίσθημα
πάντως μένει γραμμένο στὰ παμπάλαια
αὐθεντικὰ εὐαγγέλια τοῦ τρόμου μας τί ἀμοιβὴ
ὑπέρογκη ζητᾶς γιὰ τὴν ἀθανασία σου:
τὴ θνητότητά μας
(μεγάλος συκοφάντης σου μὰ καὶ ὑποστηρικτής σου).
Θέλεις ἐσὺ νὰ εἶσαι ὁ ἐκβραχιστὴς
τῆς σφηνωμένης μέσα μας ἀγάπης
γιὰ τὴ ζωὴ ποὺ ἦταν ὅπως λὲς ἔμπνευση δική σου.

Ἄραγε τί τὸν θὲς τὸ θάνατό μας
νὰ σοῦ φυλάει τί, δεμένος ἔξω ἀπ' τ' ὄνομά σου,
τί ποὺ φοβᾶσαι μὴν σ' τὸ κλέψει ἡ νόησή μας.

Μὲ ποιὸ μέσον ἐρχόμαστε στὸν κόσμο
δὲν φαίνεται νὰ σὲ πολυσκοτίζει

THE UNPROVEN IS INNOCENT

Lord, I know,
again I dig up roads already dug—
many exploratory anxieties
bowed more deeply over them long before I did.
Unshakeable is the kingdom of the unproven
(your great slanderer but also your supporter).

I want to find out whether our faith drove you to taste
the succulent office of the Culprit
only slightly to weaken the Inexplicable.

Whether or not you were involved in the slip of omnipotence,
in our terror's ancient
authentic gospels remains inscribed
the exorbitant price you demand for your immortality:
our mortality
(your great slanderer but also your supporter).
You want to be the extractor
of the rock—jammed into us—of love
for life, which you say was your own idea.

Why do you need our death, I wonder,
what do you want it to guard, tethered to your name,
what do you fear our intellect might steal?

How we come into the world
does not seem to worry you too much,

τὸ ἀναθέτεις σὲ πλανόδιες αἰτίες.

Ἄλλους μᾶς φέρνει ἕνα φιλὶ
στὸ κρύο μέτωπο τῆς πλήξης, μερικοὺς
μᾶς ξετρυπώνει ὁ ἔρωτας κρυμμένους
στὰ βάθη τῶν κινδύνων του νὰ σβήσει,
ἄλλων μιὰ μνήμη εἶναι ὁ κομιστὴς
κι ὅλους μαζὶ θαρρεῖς πὼς μᾶς γεννᾶ
ὁ τρόμος τοῦ θανάτου.

Σκάβω μήπως δὲν εἶσαι τόσο ἄθεος.
Μὴ στάθηκες κι ἐσὺ πρόωρος αἰσιόδοξος σὰν ὅλους:
ἔπλασες τὸν κόσμο πρὶν χρειαστεῖ νὰ κλάψεις.

Λίγο σὲ ἀθωώνει αὐτὴ ἡ σκέψη.
Ὅπως ἀθωώνει πρὸς στιγμὴν τὸ φεγγάρι
μόλις φανεῖ
τὴν τόση σκοτεινότητα τριγύρω.
Σχεδὸν τὴν ἐξυμνεῖ.

you delegate this to itinerant causes.

Some of us are brought here by a kiss
on boredom's cold brow, some
are unearthed by love while hidden
deep in the danger of its extinction,
others are borne hither by a memory —
you'd think we were all begotten
by the fear of death.

I dig in case you're not such an atheist.
In case you prove a premature optimist like everyone else —
creating the world before you needed to cry.

This thought hardly exonerates you.
As for a moment, when the moon appears,
it exonerates
all the surrounding darkness.
Almost extolling it.

ΜΕΓΑΛΗ ΠΕΜΠΤΗ

Ὑπαίθριος καιρός.
Κάτι ἐλιὲς πᾶνε νὰ μαζέψουν ἀνήφορο.
Φορτωμένες.
Ὁ καρπὸς εἰσακούστηκε τὸ παρελθέτω ὄχι.
Δὲν θὰ εἰσπράξουν οὔτε φέτος πατέρες
οἱ λιποψυχίες μας.

Ἀτελὴς ἡ ἐλαιογραφία.
Νὰ ξαναδοκιμάσω.

Κάτι ἐλιὲς πᾶνε νὰ μαζέψουν ἀνήφορο.
Τὰ ἀργύρια φύλλα τους ἐποφθαλμιᾶ
ἡ ἀστραφτερὴ τοῦ τοπίου ἁγνότητα.
Φύσει καταδότρια ἡ ἀθωότης.
Αὐτὴ δὲν μᾶς παρέδωσε
γιὰ ἐλάχιστα ἀνεκπλήρωτα ἀργύρια
στὴν ἀπώλειά της;

Νὰ τονίσω λίγο Φαρισαῖον ἀπέναντι.
Τὴ θάλασσα.

HOLY THURSDAY

Outdoor weather.
Some olive trees harvest their way up the mountain.
Overloaded.
The fruit has been granted, the *pass-from-me* not.
This year again, disheartenment
will earn us no fathers.

The oil painting's not right.
Let me try again.

Some olive trees harvest their way up the mountain.
The landscape's radiant chastity
covets the silver of their leaves.
Innocence is by nature a traitor.
Did it not hand us over
for a few pieces of unredeemed silver
to its own loss?

Let me add a touch of Pharisee just opposite:
the sea.

ΥΠΟΚΑΤΑΣΤΑΤΟ

Σκορπίζουν
τῶν δακρύων οἱ μεγάλες συγκεντρώσεις.
Μνήμη καὶ παρὸν ψάχνουν νὰ κρυφτοῦν
ἀπὸ τὴ διαύγειά τους.

Ἀραιὰ καὶ ποῦ καμιὰ τουφεκιὰ
πότε ἀπὸ κεῖνο τὸ εὐκρινὲς
χαράκωμα ἢ λύπη πότε ἀπὸ ἀμυδρότερο.
Στρατηγικὴ νὰ δείξει τάχα
ὅτι ἔρχονται ἐνισχύσεις.
        Ἂς παραδοθεῖ.

Ἔχει σχεδὸν ἐπικρατήσει ἡ φωτογραφία σου.
Ἐξαπλώθηκε ὅπου βρῆκε ἄμαχη ἐπιφάνεια
ἀποδεκατισμένη αἴσθηση πρόθυμη γιὰ γαλήνη.
Ἀνεμίζει στῶν βλεμμάτων τὰ ὑψώματα
ὄχι σὰν ἔθιμο ἀδρανὲς μελαγχολικὸ
μὰ ὡς γενναῖος συκοφάντης τῆς ἀπώλειάς σου.
Μέρα τὴ μέρα πείθει πὼς τίποτα δὲν ἄλλαξε
ὅτι ἤσουν πάντα ἔτσι, ἀπὸ χαρτὶ
ἐκ γενετῆς φωτογραφία σὲ συνάντησα
ἀνέκαθεν πὼς ἔτσι σ᾽ ἀγαποῦσα γυρολόγα
ἀπὸ εἰκόνα σὲ ἀπεικόνιση
κι ἀπὸ ἀπεικόνιση σὲ εἰκόνα σου ἀρκέστηκα.

Μνήμη καὶ παρὸν πρέπει νὰ κρυφτοῦν
ἀπὸ τὴ διαύγειά τους.

•

SUBSTITUTE

Scattered,
the grand gatherings of tears.
Memory and the present seek to flee
their lucidity.

Once in a while a rifle shot
from Sorrow's now distinct
now more vague trench.
A stratagem to suggest
reinforcements are coming.

                               May she surrender.

Your photograph has almost prevailed,
having spread wherever it found a civilian area,
a sensation so decimated as to seek peace.
Waving from the heights of glances
not as an effete melancholy custom
but as a brave slanderer decrying your loss.
Day after day it's convincing: nothing's changed,
that's how you always were, made of paper,
a photograph from birth, that's how I met you
and have always loved you, like a peddler I've gone
from picture to depiction
and with your picture and depiction I've contented myself.

Memory and the present have to flee
their lucidity.

•

Ἀραιὰ καὶ ποῦ καμιὰ τουφεκιὰ ἀμυδρὴ
μαρτυρία ὑπέρ σου ἡ λύπη
ἂς παραδοθεῖ.

Ὁ μόνος ἀξιόπιστος μάρτυρας ὅτι ζήσαμε
εἶναι ἡ ἀπουσία μας.

Once in a while a rifle shot, vague
evidence in your defense, from Sorrow

                                 may she surrender.

The only reliable witness to our life
is our absence.

ΚΟΝΙΑΚ ΜΗΔΕΝ ΑΣΤΕΡΩΝ

Χαμένα πᾶνε ἐντελῶς τὰ λόγια τῶν δακρύων.
Ὅταν μιλάει ἡ ἀταξία ἡ τάξη νὰ σωπαίνει
— ἔχει μεγάλη πεῖρα ὁ χαμός.
Τώρα πρέπει νὰ σταθοῦμε στὸ πλευρὸ
τοῦ ἀνώφελου.
Σιγὰ σιγὰ νὰ ξαναβρεῖ τὸ λέγειν της ἡ μνήμη
νὰ δίνει ὡραῖες συμβουλὲς μακροζωίας
σὲ ὅ,τι ἔχει πεθάνει.

Ἂς σταθοῦμε στὸ πλευρὸ ἐτούτης τῆς μικρῆς
φωτογραφίας
ποὺ εἶναι ἀκόμα στὸν ἀνθὸ τοῦ μέλλοντός της:
νέοι ἀνώφελα λιγάκι ἀγκαλιασμένοι
ἐνώπιον ἀνωνύμως εὐθυμούσης παραλίας.
Ναύπλιο Εὔβοια Σκόπελος;
Θὰ πεῖς
καὶ ποῦ δὲν ἦταν τότε θάλασσα.

ZERO STAR BRANDY

The tears' words get completely lost.
When disorder speaks, order must keep silent
—loss has great experience.
Now we must stand by
pointlessness.
So that memory gradually may regain its eloquence
and give good counsel on longevity
to all that has died.

Let's stand by this little
photograph
that's still in the bloom of its future:
young people somewhat pointlessly embracing one another
in front of an anonymously cheerful beach.
Nauplion Euboea Skopelos?
You'll say
where wasn't there sea back then.

Η ΕΦΗΒΕΙΑ ΤΗΣ ΛΗΘΗΣ (1994)

OBLIVION'S ADOLESCENCE (1994)

Η ΕΦΗΒΕΙΑ ΤΗΣ ΛΗΘΗΣ

Περιμένω λίγο
νὰ σκουρήνουν οἱ διαφορὲς καὶ τ' ἀδιάφορα
κι ἀνοίγω τὰ παράθυρα. Δὲν ἐπείγει
ἀλλὰ τὸ κάνω ἔτσι γιὰ νὰ μὴ σκεβρώσει ἡ κίνηση.
Δανείζομαι τὸ κεφάλι τῆς πρώην περιέργειάς μου
καὶ τὸ περιστρέφω. Ὄχι ἀκριβῶς περιστρέφω.
Καλησπερίζω δουλικὰ ὅλους αὐτοὺς τοὺς κόλακες
τῶν φόβων, τὰ ἀστέρια. Ὄχι ἀκριβῶς καλησπερίζω.
Στερεώνω μὲ βλεμμάτινη κλωστὴ
τ' ἀσημένια κουμπάκια τῆς ἀπόστασης
κάποια ποὺ ἔχουν ξηλωθεῖ τρέμουνε καὶ θὰ πέσουν.
Δὲν ἐπείγει. Τὸ κάνω μόνο γιὰ νὰ δείξω στὴν ἀπόσταση
πόσο εὐγνωμονῶ τὴν προσφορά της.

Ἂν δὲν ὑπῆρχε ἡ ἀπόσταση
θὰ μαραζώνανε τὰ μακρινὰ ταξίδια
μὲ μηχανάκι θὰ μᾶς ἔφερναν στὰ σπίτια
σὰν πίτσες τὴν ὑφήλιο ποὺ ὀρέχτηκε ἡ φυγή μας.
Θὰ ἤτανε σὰν βδέλλες κολλημένα
πάνω στὰ νιάτα τὰ γεράματα
καὶ θὰ μὲ φώναζαν γιαγιὰ ἀπ' τὰ χαράματά μου
ἐγγόνια μου καὶ ἔρως ἀδιακρίτως.
καὶ τί θὰ ἦταν τ' ἄστρα
δίχως τὴν ὑποστήριξη ποὺ τοὺς παρέχει ἡ ἀπόσταση.
Ἐπίγεια ἀσημικά, τίποτα κηροπήγια τασάκια
νὰ ρίχνει ἐκεῖ τὶς στάχτες του ὁ ἀρειμάνιος πλοῦτος
νὰ ἐπενδύει ὁ θαυμασμὸς τὴν ὑπερτίμησή του.

•

OBLIVION'S ADOLESCENCE

I wait awhile
for the darkening of differences and indifferences
and I open the windows. There's no rush,
still I do it to keep motion from warping.
I borrow the head of my lapsed curiosity
and rotate it. No, not quite rotate.
Slavishly I nod good evening to all those toadies of fears,
the stars. No, not quite good evening.
With eyesight thread I stitch in place
the silver buttons of Distance
that have come loose, are dangling, and will fall.
There's no rush. I do it only to show Distance
my deep appreciation for its gifts.

If not for Distance
journeys to faraway lands would wizen,
the universe our fleeing craved
would be delivered like pizza on motorbikes.
Onto youth old age
would latch like a leech,
and from my first dawn the name I'd hear would be Grandma
from Love and my grandchildren alike.
What would the stars be
without the help of Distance?
Earthly flatware, candlestick ashtrays
in which chain-smoking Wealth could tip his ash
in which Admiration could invest her overestimates.

•

Ἂν δὲν ὑπῆρχε ἡ ἀπόσταση
στὸν ἑνικὸ θὰ μᾶς μιλοῦσε ἡ νοσταλγία.
Οἱ σπάνιες τώρα ντροπαλές της συναντήσεις
μὲ τὴν πληθυντικὴ ἀνάγκη μας
μοιραῖα τότε θ' ἀφομοίωναν
τὴν ἀλανιάρα γλώσσα τῆς συχνότητας.

Βέβαια, ἂν δὲν ὑπῆρχε ἡ ἀπόσταση
δὲν θά 'τανε σὰν ἄστρο μακρινὸ ἐκεῖνος ὁ πλησίον
θὰ 'ρχόταν στὴν πρωτεύουσα προσέγγιση
μόνο δυὸ βήματα θ' ἀπέχανε τὰ ὄνειρα
ἀπὸ τὴ σκιαγράφησή του.
Ὅπως κοντά μας θὰ παρέμενε
ἡ ὕστατη φευγάλα τῆς ψυχῆς.
Πρὸς τί ἡ τόση περιπλάνηση. Χῶρος
κενὸς ὑπάρχει. Ἐμεῖς θὰ κατεβαίναμε
νὰ ζήσουμε στὸ ὑπόγειο κορμί μας
κι ἐκείνη μὲ τὸ μύθο της καὶ τὰ συμπράγκαλά του
θὰ μετεμψυχωνότανε σὲ σῶμα.

Ἂν δὲν ὑπῆρχες ἐσὺ ἀπόσταση
θὰ πέρναγε πολὺ εὐκολότερα
πιὸ γρήγορα ἐν μιᾶ νυκτὶ ἡ λήθη
τὴ δύσκολη παρατεταμένη ἐφηβεία της
αὐτὸ ποὺ χάριν εὐφωνίας ὀνομάζουμε μνήμη.

Ὄχι ἀκριβῶς μνήμη. Στερεώνω
μὲ βλεμμάτινη κλωστὴ ὁμοιώσεις

If not for Distance
Nostalgia would address us as her chum.
Her now infrequent, timid rendezvous
with our daily needs
would have to assimilate
frequency's vulgar tongue.

Surely, if not for Distance,
your fellow man would not be like a distant star
he would approach so closely
dreams would be only two steps away
from his silhouette.
Just as the Soul's final way out
would stay near us.
Why all this wandering? There's still
open space. We would go underneath
and live inside our subterranean skin
while the Soul and her myth and all its junk
would be born again as a body.

Distance, if you did not exist,
it would be far easier
for Oblivion swiftly, in a single night,
to pass through her troublesome extended adolescence
which, for the sake of euphony, we call memory.

No, not quite memory. With my eyesight thread
I stitch in place likenesses

ἔχουν ξηλωθεῖ τρέμουνε καὶ θὰ πέσουν.

Ὄχι ἀκριβῶς στερεώνω. Δουλικὰ περιστρέφομαι
γύρω ἀπ' αὐτοὺς τοὺς κόλακες τοῦ χρόνου ποὺ
χάριν συντομίας τοὺς ὀνόμασα μνήμη.

Ὄχι ἀκριβῶς μνήμη. Ἀνεφοδιάζω διάττοντες
μὲ παρατεταμένη ἐκμηδένιση. Ἐπείγει.

that have come loose, are dangling, and will fall.
Not quite stitch. Slavishly I circle
these toadies of time
for the sake of brevity I called memory.
Not quite memory. I fuel shooting stars
with extended annihilation. There is a rush.

ΤΟ ΣΠΑΝΙΟ ΔΩΡΟ

Καινούργιες θεωρίες.
Τὰ μωρὰ δὲν πρέπει νὰ τ' ἀφήνετε νὰ κλαῖνε.
Ἀμέσως νὰ τὰ παίρνετε ἀγκαλιά. Ἀλλιῶς
ὑπόκειται σὲ πρόωρη ἀνάπτυξη
τὸ αἴσθημα ἐγκατάλειψης ἐνηλικιώνεται
ἀφύσικα τὸ παιδικό τους τραῦμα
βγάζει δόντια μαλλιὰ νύχια γαμψὰ μαχαίρια.

Γιὰ τοὺς μεγάλους, οὕτως εἰπεῖν τοὺς γέροντες
—ὅ,τι δὲν εἶναι ἄνοιξη εἶναι γερόντιο πιὰ—
ἰσχύουν πάντα οἱ παμπάλαιες ἀπόψεις.
Ποτὲ ἀγκαλιά. Ἀφῆστε τους να σκάσουνε στὸ κλάμα
μέχρι νὰ τοὺς κοπεῖ ἡ ἀνάσα
δυναμώνουν ἔτσι τὰ ἀποσιωπητικά τους.
Ἂς κλαῖνε οἱ μεγάλοι. Δὲν ἔχει ἀγκαλιά.
Γεμίστε μοναχὰ τὸ μπιμπερό τους
μὲ ἄγλυκην ὑπόσχεση —δὲν κάνει νὰ παχαίνουν
οἱ στερήσεις— πὼς θά 'ρθει μία καὶ καλὴ
νὰ τοὺς ἐπικοιμήσει λιπόσαρκα
ἡ ἀγκαλιὰ τῆς μάνας τους.
Βάλτε κοντά τους τὸ μηχάνημα ἐκεῖνο
ποὺ καταγράφει τοὺς θορύβους τοῦ μωροῦ
ὥστε ν' ἀκοῦτε ἀπὸ μακριὰ
ἂν εἶναι ρυθμικὰ μοναχικὴ ἡ ἀναπνοή τους.
Ποτὲ μὴ γελαστεῖτε νὰ τοὺς πάρετε ἀγκαλιά.
Τυλίγονται ἄγρια
γύρω ἀπ' τὸν σπάνιο λαιμὸ αὐτοῦ τοῦ δώρου,

THE RARE GIFT

New theories.
Don't leave babies alone to cry.
Immediately take them into your arms. Or else
the sense of abandonment
develops prematurely,
their childhood trauma unnaturally comes of age,
grows teeth hair crooked nails knives.

For adults, the aged so to speak
—whatever isn't spring is already aged—
the ancient ways still prevail.
Never into your arms. Let them cry their hearts out
till their lungs burst,
it strengthens their muteness
Let the aged cry. No arms allowed.
Just fill their bottle
with an unsweetened promise—privation mustn't get fat—
that fleshlessly they'll be cradled
once and for all
in their mother's arms.
In their vicinity put a machine
that monitors a baby's sounds
to be sure you can hear from a distance
if their breathing has a lonely rhythm.
Never be tricked into taking them into your arms.
Fiercely they'll coil
around the neck of this rare gift,

θὰ σᾶς πνίξουν.

Τίποτα. Ὅταν σᾶς ζητᾶνε ἀγκαλιὰ
μολὼν λαβὲ μωρό μου, μολὼν λαβὲ νὰ ἀπαντᾶτε.

they'll choke you.

Forget it. When they ask to be taken into your arms
reply, *come and get them, baby, come and get them.*

ΣΑΝ ΝΑ ΔΙΑΛΕΞΕΣ

Παρασκευὴ εἶναι σήμερα θὰ πάω στὴ λαϊκὴ
νὰ κάνω ἕναν περίπατο στ' ἀποκεφαλισμένα περιβόλια
νὰ δῶ τὴν εὐωδιὰ τῆς ρίγανης
σκλάβα σὲ ματσάκια.

Πάω μεσημεράκι ποὺ πέφτουν οἱ τιμὲς τῶν ἀξιώσεων
βρίσκεις τὸ πράσινο εὔκολο
σὲ φασολάκια κολοκύθια μολόχες καὶ κρινάκια.
Ἀκούω ἐκεῖ τί θαρρετὰ ἐκφράζονται τὰ δέντρα
μὲ τὴν κομμένη γλώσσα τῶν καρπῶν
ρήτορες σωροὶ τὰ πορτοκάλια καὶ τὰ μῆλα
καὶ παίρνει νὰ ροδίζει λίγη ἀνάρρωση
στὶς κιτρινιάρικες παρειὲς
μιᾶς μέσα βουβαμάρας.

Σπάνια νὰ ψωνίσω. Γιατὶ ἐκεῖ σοῦ λένε *διάλεξε*.
Εἶναι εὐκολία αὐτὴ ἢ πρόβλημα; Διαλέγεις καὶ μετὰ
πῶς τὸ σηκώνεις τὸ βάρος τὸ ἀσήκωτο
ποὺ ἔχει ἡ ἐκλογή σου.
Ἐνῶ ἐκεῖνο τὸ ἔτυχε τί πούπουλο. Στὴν ἀρχή.
Γιατὶ μετὰ σὲ γονατίζουν οἱ συνέπειες.
Ἀσήκωτες κι αὐτές.
Κατὰ βάθος εἶναι σὰν νὰ διάλεξες.

Τὸ πολὺ ν' ἀγοράσω λίγο χῶμα. Ὄχι γιὰ λουλούδια.
Γιὰ ἐξοικείωση.
Ἐκεῖ δὲν ἔχει *διάλεξε*. Ἐκεῖ μὲ κλειστὰ τὰ μάτια.

AS IF YOU'D CHOSEN

Today's Friday I'll go to the market square
to stroll through the decapitated gardens
to see the aroma of oregano
enslaved in small bunches.

I go around noon when the price of expectations
is falling, you find the green
of string beans zucchinis mallows and lilies affordable.
Over there I hear how boldly the trees express themselves
in the cut-off tongue of fruit
—heaps and piles of orators the oranges and apples—
and a slight recovery starts turning slowly rosy
on the sallow cheeks
of an internal muteness.

I rarely purchase anything. Because there they tell you *choose*.
Does this make things easier or is it a problem? You choose and then
how do you bear the unbearable weight
of your choice?
Whereas the *it-happened-so*—a feather. At first.
Later the consequences bring you to your knees.
Also unbearable.
Deep down it's as if you'd chosen.

At most I buy some soil. Not for flowers.
Just to familiarize myself.
No *choosing* there. There it's with eyes closed.

ΚΑΤΩΤΕΡΑ ΤΑΞΙΣ

III

Ἀηδόνια ξεναγοῦν τὴν ἀκοὴ
στὰ ψηφιδωτὰ τοῦ Μάη ἀγριολούλουδα.

Τὸ Ἡραῖον, Ἡ ἐξέδρα τοῦ Ἡρώδη, Τὸ Πρυτανεῖον.
Δὲς τί προϊστορία κατατρόπωσε μιὰ σταλιὰ παρόν.

Πολιτισμοὶ καὶ τύμβοι τῆς δυσαναλογίας
ἄνω κάτω μέσα στὸ μυαλό μου.

Ξεχνῶ σὲ ποιὸ χαμό τους στρατοπέδευσαν
τόσες ἐπιφανεῖς χρονολογίες
πότε ἀνακηρύχθηκε ἀπώτερος σκοπὸς ἡ ἐξουσία
συγχέω πάντα ὅσα ἔγιναν πρὸ τῆς ὑπάρξεώς μου
μὲ τὸ σὰν νὰ μὴν ἔγιναν. Μετὰ τὴν ὕπαρξή μας
νὰ μοῦ τὸ θυμηθεῖς
ἐτούτη μου ἡ σύγχυση θ᾽ ἀποδειχτεῖ προφήτης.

Κατανοῶ εὐκολότερα
τὶς διασκορπισμένες ὁλόγυρα πέτρες
ὅπως τὶς ἔφερε ἀνώνυμες στὸ φῶς ἡ ἀνασκαφὴ
τμήματα κάποιας ἀρτιότητας ποὺ
ἄγνωστο σὲ τί κατώτερά της
στρώματα χώματος ὑπέπεσε.
Μοῦ εἶναι οἰκεῖο τὸ χαμένο νόημά τους.
Τὶς παρηγορῶ ἐπιγράφοντάς τες
ὅπως ἐπιγράφουν οἱ κινήσεις τῶν κλαδιῶν

LOWER CLASS

III

Nightingales guide my hearing
through May's wildflower mosaic.

The Temple of Hera, the Nymphaeum of Herodes, the Prytaneion.
See how much prehistory a tiny bit of the present has crushed.

Disproportion's civilizations and tombs
are topsy-turvy in my mind.
I forget in which of their annihilations
so many illustrious dates made their camps,
when power was proclaimed the ultimate goal,
I always confuse whatever happened prior to my existence
with as-if-it-hadn't-happened. After we cease to exist
mark my words
my confusion will prove prophetic.

I better comprehend
the stones scattered all around
as they were, anonymous, brought to light by the excavation,
parts of some wholeness—
no one knows which lower level
of earth it went under.
To me their lost meaning is familiar.
I comfort them by inscribing them
as the branches' faint movements inscribe

ἀχνὲς τὸν σκόρπιο ἀνοιξιάτικο ἀέρα:

Ἀπόσπασμα δραπέτη δούλου τάφου
ἡμιτελὲς ἐπιτύμβιον ἀμούστακου θριάμβου
σκαλάκι ἐναρκτήριο μονώροφης ἑταίρας
περβάζι ἀπὸ παράθυρο ποὺ ἔλιαζε τὴ γλάστρα της
ἐνάρετη πλατύφυλλη ἑστία
καὶ τούτη δῶ ποὺ κάθομαι
πεζοδρόμιο ἐντόμων καὶ σκιερῶν εἰκασιῶν.

Ἀλήθεια ποῦ νὰ κεῖνται σκόρπιες
ἀνεπίγραφες οἱ δικές μου ἧττες.
Πολεμώντας νικήθηκα ἢ διαβαίνοντας;

Ὀλυμπία

the scattered spring air:

Fragment of a fugitive slave tomb
unfinished epitaph of a beardless triumph
small lowest stair of a one-story hetaera
windowsill on which a virtuous large-leafed home
was sunning its flowerpot
and this one here I'm sitting on—
a sidewalk for insects and shadowy conjectures.

Where would my own uninscribed defeats
lie scattered, I wonder.
Was I defeated while fighting or while passing by?

Olympia

ΡΑΝΤΕΒΟΥ ΜΕ ΜΙΑΝ ΑΓΝΩΣΤΗ

Τί θὰ φορᾶς συνεννόησι
νὰ σὲ γνωρίσω
ὥστε νὰ μὴ χαθοῦμε πάλι
μὲς στοὺς πολυπληθεῖς σωσίες σου;

BLIND DATE

What will you wear, Agreement,
so I will know you
and we won't miss each other again
among your many doubles?

ΚΩΝΣΤΑΝΤΙΝΟΥ ΚΑΙ ΕΛΕΝΗΣ

Κύριε
σοῦ ἔφερα τὸ πρόσφορο
ζεστὴ ἀκόμα ἡ σάρξ μὲ σφραγίδα
ἐδῶ τὸ χαρτονόμισμα νὰ δώσεις κάτι στὸ κερὶ
ποὺ σοῦ διαβάζει ὀδυρμοὺς ἐν περιλήψει
κι ἐδῶ εἶναι τὸ χαρτὶ μὲ τῶν ψυχῶν τὰ ὀνόματα.
Ὅσα μπορεῖς ἁγίασον.

Γιὰ τὴν Ἑλένη κυρίως ἐνδιαφέρομαι
ἤτανε κάποτε ἡ μάνα μου. Τώρα δὲν ξέρω
τί συγχωνεύσεις ἔκανες
ἂν σὲ κοινὸ αὐλάκι ῥέει
τὸ ἴδιο αἷμα μὲ τὸ ξένο
ἂν τὸ ἀδειάζεις ὡς ἀπόβλητο
ἐκεῖ ποὺ ὑδρεύονται οἱ πίστεις
ἂν τὸ ἐπεξεργάζεσαι βαφὴ γιὰ τὰ τριαντάφυλλα
βαφὴ γιὰ τὸν θυμὸ τῶν ἄλλων πραγμάτων
—νὰ ρίχνεις καμιὰ στάλα ἀπὸ δαῦτο
στὸ μαῦρο ποὺ 'ναι οἱ πληγὲς— αἷμα δικό τους εἶναι.

Ἑλένη. Νὰ σ' τὴν δείξω μὴν τὴν μπερδέψεις
μὲ ἄλλες ἔτσι ποὺ κατάργησες τὰ ἐπίθετα
κατάργησες τὶς ἀνομοιότητες.
Μόνο διακριτικὸ ποὺ τοὺς ἀπέμεινε
εἶναι πόσο τοὺς ξέχασαν
καὶ πόσο ἀκόμα τοὺς θυμοῦνται.
Ἀλλὰ αὐτὸ ἐσένα μᾶλλον σὲ μπερδεύει.

SAINT CONSTANTINE AND SAINT HELEN'S DAY

Lord,
I brought you an altar bread
its flesh still warm, with the seal.
Here is the money to pay the candle
that reads abbreviated lamentations to you
and here is the paper with the souls' names.
Please bless as many as you can.

It's Helen I'm most interested in
she was my mother once. Now I don't know
what mixtures you have made—
if one's own and the alien blood
flow together in a common ditch
if you empty it as waste
where faiths draw their water
if you transform it into a dye for roses
a dye for the wrath of immaterial things—
in order to pour a droplet
on the blackness that wounds are—it's their own blood after all.

Helen. Let me show her to you so you won't confuse her
with the others since you've abolished surnames
abolished dissimilarities.
The only distinctive mark that remains to them
is how much they've been forgotten
and how much they're still remembered.
Maybe this confuses you.

Τὸ ἔργο σου ἐσὺ τὸ ἀναγνωρίζεις
ἀπ' τὸ εὐδιάκριτο ἐκεῖνο ἀδιακρίτως.

Ἑλένη Ἑλένη — ἄσε τὸν Ἀθανάσιον
τὸν ἔχω ἀναλάβει ἐγὼ αὐτὸν
τὸν ἀναπαύω ἐγὼ αὐτὸν σὲ πουπουλένια κλάματα.
Τὴ μάνα μου ἁγίασον.

Ἔλα πιὸ κάτω νὰ σ' τὴν δείξω.
Εἶναι ἐκείνη ἡ συρμάτινη φουρκέτα.
Διχαλωτὴ αἰωρεῖται σὰν κεραῖες
σβησμένου ἀποτυπώματος μικροῦ σαλιγκαριοῦ.

Ἔτσι ἔζησαν τὰ λιγοστὰ μαλλιά της.
Γυροφέρνοντας τὸ σχῆμα ἑνὸς κότσου
ἴδιος μὲ ἀσθενικὸ σαλιγκαριοῦ καβούκι
ποὺ ὅλο ξεγλιστροῦσαν καὶ κατέρρεαν
ἀδύναμοι οἱ κύκλοι του ἀπ' τὴν περιέλιξή τους.
Καὶ ἡ φουρκέτα — συνέχισε μάνα γιὰ λίγο ἐσὺ
νὰ τρέξω ἐγὼ νὰ πιάσω τὸν κρυφτούλη ἦχο
τῆς πτώσης ἄφθαρτα ὅπως χτυπᾶ
ἐπάνω στὴν πλακόστρωτη τὴν πατρικὴ ἐπιφάνειά μου.

Αὐτὴ εἶναι, δές την καλά.
Κοίτα μὴ μοῦ ἁγιάσεις ξένη μάνα
καὶ γίνει τώρα ἡ στοργικὴ ὀρφάνια μου
μετὰ ἀπὸ τόσα χρόνια μητριά μου.

You recognize your work
by its distinct indiscriminateness.

Helen Helen—don't worry about Athanasios
I'm taking care of him
I have him resting on a featherbed of tears.
Bless my mother.

Come farther down and I'll show her to you.
She is this wire hairpin
forked, dangling, like the tentacles
of a small snail's obliterated imprint.

So lived her sparse hairs.
Winding their way around the shape of a bun
resembling a snail's fragile shell,
their frail coils always slipping and sliding
out of circumvolution.
And the hairpin—you take over a moment, Mother,
while I run to catch the small hidden sound
of its fall as it imperishably strikes
the paved surface of my father's house.

She's the one, take a good look at her.
Be careful not to bless some alien mother
for fear that, after all these years, my loving orphanhood
will become my stepmother.

Μετὰ τὰ *Ποιήματα*

After *Poems*

ΕΝΟΣ ΛΕΠΤΟΥ ΜΑΖΙ (1998)

A MOMENT OF TWO (1998)

ΕΠΕΙΣΟΔΙΟ

Τότε ποὺ ἡ γλώσσα μὲ δασύτριχες
ἄναρθρες κραυγὲς χτυποῦσε
τὴν πήλινη καμπάνα τοῦ οὐρανίσκου
κι εὔληπτη ὡστόσο ἀντιλαλοῦσε ἡ ἐπιβίωση

ἢ τὰν ἢ ἐπὶ τᾶς

χαράματα ξεκίναγε ἡ πεῖνα
γιὰ τὸ κυνήγι τοῦ ἀβέβαιου

κι εἴθε νὰ γύριζε νικήτρια
αἱμάσσοντας ἡ πλάτη της ἀγρίμι
στοῦ βέλους τὸ φαρμάκι κρεμασμένο

κι ὡσότου νὰ χορέψει ἄγρια ἡ πρόγευση
γύρω ἀπὸ τὴ γδαρμένη προστασία τῆς προβιᾶς
σουρούπωνε ἀθώα ἡ ὠμότης
κι ὀρεκτικὸ σιγοψηνότανε τὸ βράδυ
στῶν ἀστεριῶν τὴ θράκα

τόσο λιτὰ χανότανε ἡ μέρα.

Ἀλλεπάλληλοι τότε οἱ σεισμοὶ καθὼς
ἡ ὀγκώδης στρογγυλότητα τῆς γῆς
ταπεινωμένη ἀντιστεκόταν
νὰ ἰσορροπήσει ἐπάνω στὸ λεπτότατο
νεοφερμένο τῆς ὑπάρξεώς μας νῆμα.

•

INCIDENT

Back when the tongue was striking
the palate's earthen bell
producing hairy inarticulate cries
back when survival nonetheless reverberated intelligibly:

either with this or on this

hunger would set off at dawn
to go hunting for uncertainty

may it return victorious
its back bloody, some wild beast
hanging from the arrow's poison

and while the foretaste danced wildly
around the fleece's skinned protection,
innocent rawness was setting,
the evening slowly roasting as an appetizer
on embers of the stars

so simple was the day's fading.

Successive earthquakes ensued because
the earth's massive roundness
—humiliated—balked
at balancing on the new
slender thread of our existence.

•

Σεισμὸς λογίζονταν κι ὁ ἔρωτας
μὲ ἀνόητο ἐπίκεντρο τὸ σῶμα
μὰ ποὺ γινόταν ἔκθαμβα αἰσθητὸς
καὶ στὶς θαμμένες περιοχὲς τῆς εὐτυχίας
καὶ στῆς ἀπώτερης σπορᾶς μας τοὺς ἀγρούς.

Σβηστὸ ἀκόμα τὸ ἠφαίστειο τῆς ἅμιλλας.
Καλύτερος μονάχα ὁ ἐπιζῶν
κι ἀπαρατήρητος τρελὸς ἐκεῖνος ποὺ
χάραζε σὲ βράχους τὸ σχῆμα τῆς τροφῆς του
— ζῶα καὶ φόβο μὴ χαθοῦν.
Γαλήνιο πολίτευμα ἡ ἀφάνεια.
Ὥσπου ροβόλησαν ἀπὸ τὸ ἀναπάντεχο
οἱ ταραξίες λέξεις διεφθαρμένοι κανταδόροι
παίζοντας ὕμνο δόλιο.

Πρώτη χαιρέτησε ἡ μουσικότης
ὕστερα μίλησε ἡ ἀγάπη ἀναπτύσσοντας
διὰ μακρῶν τὶς φυλακές της
μὲ τοὺς ἐλάχιστους κρατούμενους
κάπου στὰ μισὰ τῆς λειτουργίας
ἔβγαλε δίσκο ἡ ἰσότης
καὶ τελευταία καταπέλτης
ἡ φτιαξιὰ τοῦ καθενός μας προστάζοντας
τοὺς ζυγοὺς λύσατε.

Οἱ λέξεις φταῖνε. Αὐτὲς
ἐνθάρρυναν τὰ πράγματα σιγὰ

Love too was considered an earthquake
—the body its silly epicenter—
dazzlingly felt
both in the buried areas of happiness
and in the fields of our ultimate sowing.

Still dormant competition's volcano.
Best of all men was the survivor who just scraped by,
and an inconspicuous madman, he who
carved on rocks the shape of his food
—animals and the fear of losing them.
The obscure—a peaceful regime.
Until troublemaking words rumbled down
from the unexpected—corrupt singers
playing a deceitful hymn.

The first to salute was musicality
then love gave a lengthy speech elaborating on
its prisons
with their scant detainees,
somewhere in the middle of Mass
equality passed the plate
and last our character
—a catapult—commanding:
break ranks.

Blame the words. They
prompted things

σιγὰ ν' ἀρχίσουν νὰ συμβαίνουν.

Πρωτύτερα ὁ θάνατος τί ἦταν;
Μιὰ στάθμευση πολύωρη μαυρίλας
πάνω στὶς ράγες τοῦ φωτὸς.

Μαλάκιο ἀηδὲς ἡ ματαιότης.
Μιλώντας μεγαλοπιάστηκε
κι ἔλαβε σάρκα καὶ ὀστὰ ποὺ
τὰ ἀφαιρεῖ βεβαίως ἀπὸ μᾶς
κάθε φορὰ γιὰ νὰ ὀρθοποδήσει.

Ἄθωα δόρατα καὶ βέλη βιοπαλαιστικὰ
μιλώντας ἔγιναν Ζαῖρ Σεράγιεβο Νταχάου
— φύσει ἐκδορεὺς ἡ ἱστορία.

Πὼς ἤσουνα ἐχθρός μου δὲν τὸ ἤξερες.
Οἱ λέξεις σοῦ τὸ εἶπαν.

Σ' ἐκεῖνες πούλησε ὁ ἔρως τὸ σεισμό του
κι ἦρθε στὴν ἐπιφάνεια

ὅτι δὲν μ' ἀγαποῦσες.

Λέξεις ζηλότυπες κρυμμένες στὴν ἐκδίκηση
τῆς Μήδειας κατασφάξανε Χρυσόμαλλο
τὸ μητρικό της φίλτρο

•

to happen gradually.

What was death before that?
A prolonged stationing of blackness
on rails of light.

Vanity—a repulsive mollusk.
By speaking, it put on airs
acquired flesh and bones
each time stealing them from us of course
to stand on its own two feet.

Innocent javelins and breadwinning arrows
became Zaire Sarajevo Dachau simply by speaking
—history, by nature, flays all.

You didn't know you were my enemy.
Words told you so.

Love sold them its earthquake
and so it surfaced

that you didn't love me.

Jealous words hidden in her revenge
slaughtered, while Golden, Medea's
maternal instinct

•

μὲ λέξεις τύφλωσε ὁ Οἰδίποδας
τὶ μάνα ἐνοχή του
— λὲς καὶ δὲν εἶναι ἐκ γενετῆς
τυφλὸς ὁ πόθος

λέξεις θεάρεστες θάψανε κρυφὰ
νύκτωρ τὸν ἀδελφό τους, ἔκθετον
στὰ ὅρνια τῆς ἀτίμωσης
— λὲς καὶ θαμμένος παύει
νὰ εἶναι ἀτίμωση ὁ θάνατος

ναὶ ναί, μὲ λέξεις διαιωνίστηκε
θέατρο παγκοσμίου ἀκουστικῆς ἡ τραγωδία μας.

Καὶ ὅταν κλαῖμε μὴν ἀκοῦς
τί ψεύδονται οἱ ἀδένες
τάχα πὼς νίπτουν δάκρυα τὰς χεῖρας των.
Δὲν εἶναι δάκρυα.

Λέξεις ξαναχτυποῦν
καιρὸ ἐπιφυλαγμένες στὸ ἁλάτι τους
αὐτὲς οἱ λέξεις ἄθλιες δὲ λένε νὰ φυσήξουν
καὶ τὶ θυσία μᾶς ἐμφυσοῦν στὴν ἄπνοιά τους.

Δὲν εἶναι λέξη ὁ καιρός. Εἶναι
ὁ κακοήθης ὄγκος τῆς στιγμῆς.

with words Oedipus blinded
his mother guilt
—as if lust were not
blind at birth

by night god-pleasing words secretly buried
their brother, exposed
to dishonor's vultures
—as if death, buried, ceases
to be a dishonor

yes, yes, with words our tragedy
was perpetuated as a theater with worldwide acoustics.

And when we cry, don't listen
to the glands' lie
that supposedly tears wash their hands.
They are not tears.
Words, long cured in their own salt
are striking again—
these awful words refuse to blow
and in their stillness inspire us to sacrifice.

Time is not a word. It is
the malignant tumor of the moment.

Η ΑΝΑΤΡΟΠΗ ΤΟΥ ΕΥΛΟΓΟΥ

Προσπάθησε Θεέ μου νὰ θυμηθεῖς ποῦ ἔκρυψες
τὸ πόρισμα ἐκείνου τοῦ μεγάλου ἀτυχήματος.
Ἐμβάθυνα ὅπου ἐντόπισα θαμμένα
συντρίμμια λογικῆς
κι ἐκτὸς ἀπ' τοῦ παράλογου τοὺς ἕλικες
ποὺ ἀκόμα περιστρέφονταν ταχεῖς
ἄλλην ἐξήγηση δὲ βρῆκα.

Θέλω νὰ καταλάβω πῶς ἀνετράπη τότε ὁ κανόνας
κι ἐπῆλθε γιὰ τὸν ἄνθρωπο ἐκεῖνο τὸ μοιραῖο
κατ' ἐξαίρεσιν.

Τί ἔγινε; Ὁ δρόμος ἦταν ἴσιος.
Τὶς ἄγριες μεταξύ τους ἄναρχες διαφορὲς
ὅταν σοῦ ξεπετάχτηκαν κρυμμένες
πίσω ἀπὸ τὴ μακάρια τὴν παραδείσια ἰσότητα
τῶν ἀνθέων τῶν ἀνθέων καὶ τῶν λουλουδιῶν
τὶς πάταξες μαντρώνοντάς τες ἔξυπνα
σὲ μιὰν εὐρύχωρη διαβάθμιση
μεγάλο
μικρὸ
μικρότερο
ἐλάχιστο.
Ἔτσι τὸ μεῖζον θέμα ποιὸς θὰ τρώει ποιὸν
ρυθμίστηκε ἀπὸ τὸν νομοθέτη ὄγκο.
Ἡ πεῖνα τοῦ μεγάλου νὰ τρέφεται
μὲ τοῦ μικροῦ τὴν πεῖνα καὶ οὕτω καθεξῆς

REVERSAL OF THE REASONABLE

Try to recall, God, where you've hidden
the findings on that big accident.
I've probed deep into every scrap of buried reason
I could locate
and aside from the propellers of unreason
still spinning quickly
I found no other explanation.

I want to understand how the rule was reversed at the time
and there fell upon man that fatal
with the exception of.

What on earth happened? The course was straight.
You had smitten the wild unruly differences
among blossoms, blossoms and flowers —
when they popped up in front of you hidden
behind blissful heavenly equality —
by smartly corralling them
inside the ample gradation
big
small
smaller
smallest.
Thus the major question who would be eaten by whom
was settled by size, the legislator.
The hunger of the big was to feed
on the hunger of the small and so forth —

— ἀργότερα ἐφάνη ὅτι δὲν εἶναι καὶ τόσο εὔφορο
τὸ εὔλογο.

Κι ἐνῶ τὸ μεγάλο ψάρι ἔτρωγε τὸ μικρὸ
τὴν πεταλούδα τὸ ἐφήμερο
ὁ ἔρωτας τὸν ἔρωτα
ἡ ἐξάπλωσι τὸ μοναδικὸ
τὴν ψυχὴ ἡ ἔγνοια της ποῦ θὰ μᾶς ἀφήσει
καὶ τὰ ἑπτὰ κατσικάκια ὁ λύκος
ἐκτὸς ἀπ᾽ τὸ μικρότερο ποὺ κρύφτηκε
πίσω ἀπ᾽ τὸ παραμύθι
τί ἔγινε τελευταία στιγμὴ
σὲ τόσο ἴσιο δρόμο ποῦ χάζευες Θεέ μου
καὶ ἀνετράπη ὁ κανόνας καὶ πέσαμε
σὲ κεῖνο τὸ μοιραῖο
κατ᾽ ἐξαίρεσιν
τὸ μικρὸ σκουλήκι νὰ τρώει
τὸν μεγάλο ἄνθρωπο

ἐκτὸς ἀπ᾽ τὸν μικρότερο ποὺ κρύβεται
πίσω ἀπ᾽ τὸ παραμύθι.

later it grew clear that the reasonable
was not so regenerable.

And while the small fish was eaten by the big one
the butterfly by the ephemeral
love by love
the unique by proliferation
the soul by its worry where to leave us
and the seven lambs by the wolf
except for the smallest that hid
behind the fairy tale
what on earth happened at the last moment
on such a straight course, my God, where were you dallying
when the rule was reversed and we ran
into that fatal
with the exception of
the small worm eating
the big man

except for the smallest who hides
behind the fairy tale.

ΠΑΣΧΑ ΣΤΟ ΦΟΥΡΝΟ

Βέλαζε τὸ κατσίκι ἐπίμονα βραχνά.
Ἄνοιξα τὸ φοῦρνο μὲ θυμὸ τί φωνάζεις εἶπα
σὲ ἀκοῦνε οἱ καλεσμένοι.
Ὁ φοῦρνος σου δὲν καίει, βέλαξε
κάνε κάτι ἀλλιῶς θὰ μείνει νηστικὴ
χρονιάρα μέρα ἡ ὠμότητά σας.

Ἔβαλα μέσα τὸ χέρι μου. Πράγματι.
Παγωμένο τὸ μέτωπο τὰ πόδια ὁ σβέρκος
τὸ χορτάρι ἡ βοσκὴ τὰ κατσάβραχα
ἡ σφαγή.

EASTER IN THE OVEN

Bleating persistently, the goat went hoarse.
I opened the oven in a rage, what's all this fuss?
the guests can hear you.
Your oven's not even hot, it bleated,
do something or your raw cruelty
will be forced to fast on this festive day.

I put my hand inside. Indeed.
Everything frozen: the forehead the legs the neck
the grass the pasture the crags
the slaughter.

ΜΗΤΕΡΑ ΤΟΥ ΚΑΤΩ ΟΡΟΦΟΥ

Στὰ παιδιά μου

Ἐρρίφθη ἡ μετακόμιση κύβος ἄδειος τὸ σπίτι ἐπάνω.

Μπήκανε σὲ τεράστιες κοῦτες ἡ βελόνα κι ἡ κλωστὴ ποὺ
ἔραβε τὰ σπλάχνα βήματα τοὺς ἀπόγονους θορύβους
στὸν ποδόγυρο τῆς καθησύχασής μου—τί τέκνο στοργικὸ
τὸ καζανάκι πῶς κατέβαινε τρέχοντας τὴ νύχτα
ἐπάνω μου νὰ τὸ ἀφουγκραστῶ.

Κοῦτες δέματα μπόγοι δεθήκανε καλὰ μὲ τὸν κομμένο
ὀμφάλιο λῶρο.
Δὲ γινόταν ἄλλο δίχως ἀνελκυστήρα γκαραζ
χωρὶς βεσὲ προπάντων, ὁλόκληρη τετραμελὴς δικαιολογία
— πολὺ παλιᾶς κατασκευῆς ἡ μάνα.

Λίγες οἱ ζημιές.
Σπάσανε κάτι χρόνια μεταχειρισμένα κι ἐλάχιστα ἐπόμενα
καὶ βέβαια, θρύψαλα τὸ λάθος νὰ νομίζεις πῶς τὰ γκοοοὸλ
θὰ εἶχαν ἐσαεὶ τερματοφύλακα μόνο τὴν ἀκοή σου
ὅτι ἡ Μπάρμπι θὰ μεγάλωνε δεμένη στοὺς παραλογισμούς σου
πῶς δὲ θὰ στέρευε ποτὲ τῆς ῥὸζ κορδέλας τὸ ποτάμι

MOTHER OF THE FLOOR BELOW

To my children

The moving die's been cast—the upstairs apartment now an empty
    cube.

Packed into huge cartons the needle and thread that
sewed offspring footsteps, descendant noises
to the hem of my reassurance—water, sweet affectionate child,
running through the night and down
to me so I could hear it.

Cartons boxes bundles well-secured with the severed
umbilical cord.
It was no longer possible no elevator no garage
especially no extra bath, an entire four-membered excuse—
the mother is of very old construction.

Little was damaged.
Some used-up years were smashed as were those few to come
and shattered, of course, your mistaken belief that
goooals! would forever have your hearing as their sole goalie
Barbie would grow up attached to your irrationalities
the river of pink ribbon would never go dry

θὰ ψήλωναν στὶς ὄχθες του κι ἄλλο τὰ καταπράσινα
ποὺ φύτεψες κοτσίδια νὰ κάθονται στὸ θαλερό τους ἴσκιο
τὰ ἄσπρα σου μαλλιά.

Τὸ νόμιζες ἀκίνδυνο τὸ πειρατικὸ πλέιμομπὶλ καράβι
σὰ νὰ μὴν ἤξερες πὼς τό 'χουνε παιχνίδι νὰ φεύγουν τὰ
    οἰκεῖα
σὰ νὰ μὴν εἶχαν κι ἄλλοτε βροντήξει μὲ παιδικὴ
συναρμολογούμενη εὐκολία κανόνια καὶ πλόες
ὑπὸ ἐνήλικη σημαία.

Μαζεύω ἀπὸ χάμω παρατημένα μικροπράγματα
μὴν τὰ πατήσει ἡ ἀντήχηση καὶ σπάσω.

Μικρὲς ἀποχαιρετιστήριες μπαλίτσες κανονιοῦ
σὰ χοντρὸ πιπέρι — πιπέρι πιπέρι στὸ στόμα
στὰ κακὰ λόγια τοῦ χωρισμοῦ

τὸ νήπιο θερμόμετρο μέρες ξεχασμένο
στῆς ἱστορίας τὴν ἀπύρετη μασχάλη

τὸ πινελάκι ποὺ βάφει τὰ ματάκια της κλαμένα
ἡ κουκλίτσα λύπη
κουρέλι τὴ κόκκινη μπέρτα τοῦ Σούπερμαν.

Μὴν τὸ ἀποκλείεις. Κι ἄλλες φορὲς κουρέλι ἡ ἀντοχὴ
κι ὅμως ἀποκαλύφθηκε ὑπεράνθρωπος.

the green braids you'd planted on its banks would grow even taller
so that your white hair
would sit in their blossoming shadow.

You thought the Playmobil pirate ship was harmless
as if you didn't know that leaving is a game for intimates
as if cannons and sailings had not already thundered
with childish ease of assembly
under an adult flag.

I'm picking up abandoned odds and ends off the ground
so that the echo doesn't step on them and break me.

Tiny farewell cannonballs
like coarse pepper—pepper pepper on the tongue
against vile words of separation

the infant thermometer forgotten for days
in history's armpit, no longer feverish

the little brush with which baby-doll Sorrow
paints her eyes full of tears
the tattered red cape of Superman.

Let's not exclude that possibility. Time was when endurance,
     though in tatters,
revealed itself to be superhuman.

ΤΟΥ ΛΑΖΑΡΟΥ

Νεφοσκεπὲς ψιλόβροχο ἡμέρας.
Κάτι μωραὶ καμπάνες πιτσιλᾶνε
τὸν ὕπνο τοῦ Λαζάρου νὰ ἐξέλθει.
Καλὰ στοκαρισμένο τὸ φῶς γύρω γύρω.

Εἶχα καὶ γὼ νὰ δεῦρο κάποιους ἔξω
μὰ δὲ μοῦ ἀποκρίθηκαν ἂν θέλουν.

Πῶς ν᾽ ἀποκριθοῦν
μὲ ὠτακουστὴ ποὺ ἄφησες καλὰ στοκαρισμένο
τὸ φῶς γύρω γύρω.

Κι ἔπειτα γιατί τοὺς ρωτᾶς ἂν θέλουν.
Τὸ θαῦμα δὲ ρωτάει.
Σ᾽ ἁρπάζει ἀπὸ τὸ αὐτὶ καὶ
σέρνοντας σὲ πετάει στὸ φῶς.

Χαίρεσαι βέβαια μὲ τὴν ἔκλαμψη, δὲν ἀντιλέγω
ἀλλὰ σὲ τρώει ἀπὸ μέσα σκουλήκι ἡ ἀγωνία
μὴν εἶναι καὶ τὰ θαύματα θνητά.

Ἄστους λοιπὸν καλύτερα ἐκεῖ
μὴν ἔχωμεν νὰ ἄρωμεν γιὰ δεύτερη φορὰ
κενὸν τὸν κράββατόν τους.

SAINT LAZARUS' DAY

A day of dusky drizzle.
Some foolish bells splash
Lazarus' sleep to make it come forth.
The light is sealed tight.

I too had to make some others come forth
but they didn't say whether they wanted to.

How could they answer
in the presence of this eavesdropping light
that you left sealed tight.

Besides, why ask if they wanted to.
Miracles don't ask.
They grab you by the ear
drag you out and throw you into the light.
You rejoice in the radiance, I won't dispute that
but the worm of anxiety eats at you inside:
maybe miracles are also mortal.

Better to leave those others where they are
so we won't have to take up their beds,
empty, once more.

ΗΧΟΣ ΑΠΟΜΑΚΡΥΝΣΕΩΝ (2001)

SOUND OF DISTANCINGS (2001)

ΣΑΣ ΑΦΗΣΑ ΜΗΝΥΜΑ

Ἐμπρὸς ἐμπρὸς μὲ ἀκοῦτε; Ἐμπρὸς
ἀπὸ μακριὰ τηλεφωνῶ. Δὲν ἀκούγομαι
τί, ξεφορτίστηκε ἡ ἀπόσταση;
Ἀπὸ κινητὸ διάστημα μιλᾶτε;
Νὰ ξαναπατήσω τὸ μηδέν; Κι ἄλλο;
Μὲ ἀκοῦτε τώρα;
Ναὶ μοῦ δίνετε σᾶς παρακαλῶ τὴ μαμά μου;
Τί ἀριθμὸ πῆρα; Τὸν οὐρανὸ
αὐτὸν μοῦ ἔχουν δώσει. Δὲν εἶναι κεῖ;
Μπορῶ νὰ τῆς οὐρλιάξω ἕνα μήνυμα;
Εἶναι μεγάλη ἀνάγκη πεῖτε της
εἶδα στὸν ὕπνο μου ὅτι πέθανε κι ἐγὼ
μικρὸ παιδὶ κατουρημένο γοερὰ
μούσκεμα ὁ φόβος ὡς ἀπάνω
κι ἀκόμα νὰ στεγνώσει.

Νὰ 'ρθεῖ νὰ τὸν ἀλλάξει.

Ἂν δὲν μπορέσει, τῆς λέτε ἀκόμα ὅτι
ὡρίμασε ἐκείνη ἡ παλιὰ φοβέρα της
πὼς θὰ μὲ φάει ὁ γέρος ἂν δὲν τελειώσω
τὸ φαγητό μου.

Ὡρίμασε ἔγινα γεῦμα γήρατος.
Ὄχι σὲ ταβερνάκι ὀνείρου.
Σὲ κάποιο λαϊκὸ μαγέρικο ποὺ ἄνοιξε
ὁ καθρέφτης.

I LEFT YOU A MESSAGE

Hello hello can you hear me? Hello
I'm calling long distance. You can't hear me—
what, the distance has been discharged?
You're speaking from a mobile space?
I should press zero? Again?
Can you hear me now?
Yes, please put my mother on.
What number did I call? The sky's—
that's the one they gave me. Not there?
Can I scream a message to her?
Tell her it's extremely urgent
I dreamed she was dead and I
a small child, woefully self-pissed,
fear, drenched from head to toe,
still not completely dry.

She has to come and change it.

If she can't, tell her too
her former threat—the old man
would eat me if I didn't finish my food—
has matured.

It's matured and I've become a meal for old age.
Not in some dreamy little tavern.
In some fast-food joint opened
by the mirror.

ΑΛΗΘΙΝΗ ΑΠΑΝΤΗΣΗ

Ἀγαπητὴ φίλη

Τὸ γράμμα σου κακὸς Ἑρμῆς μαντατοφόρος.
Χρεοκοπία σου μοῦ ἀναγγέλλει.
Νὰ λυπηθῶ ἔχω νὰ σοῦ δώσω. Ἂν ὅμως μοῦ ζητᾶς
δάνειο παρηγορίας δὲ μοῦ 'χει μείνει λέξη.
Μὲ βρήκανε καὶ μένα πολλῶν λαθῶν πτωχεύσεις.

Ἤτανε λάθος σου νὰ ἀνοίξεις σὲ μία ξένη χώρα
μπουτὶκ μὲ ἀληθινὰ κοσμήματα — ἀντίγραφα περίτεχνα
αὐθεντικῆς προγόνου ἑλληνικότητας.

Ρίχνεις τὸ φταίξιμο στὰ φὸ μπιζού.

Δὲν πρόκειται γιὰ μόδα.
Εἶναι παλιὰ προτίμηση τὸ ψεύτικο.
Περίτεχνο ἀντίγραφο αὐθεντικῆς πραγματικότητας.
Τέλεια ἐπεξεργασμένο ἀπὸ τὴ μεγάλη ζήτηση.
Δὲν ἀλλοιώνεται. Ἡ ἀφθονία του ἀμετάβλητη.
Ἡ εὔκολη τιμή του τὸ κάνει προσιτὸ
σὲ κάθε μικρομεσαία πλάνη.
Καὶ νὰ τὸ χάσεις, πάλι συμφέρει
σοῦ ἔρχεται φτηνότερα νὰ κλαῖς γιὰ ἕνα ψέμα.

Ἀγανακτεῖς νὰ συνωστίζονται τόσοι θαυμαστὲς
ἀπ' ἔξω μόνο, στὴ βιτρίνα σου

REAL ANSWER

Dear Girl,

Your letter is a wicked Hermes.
It heralds your insolvency to me.

I can give you my regrets. But if you ask me
for a loan of consolation, I have none left.
I too have endured many mistakes that went bankrupt.

Yours was to open a boutique in a foreign country
with real jewelry—elaborate copies
of authentic ancestral Hellenism.

You blame fashion jewelry.

This has nothing to do with fashion.
Fake is an old preference.
An elaborate copy of authentic reality.
Perfectly gilded by great demand.
It suffers no alteration. Its abundance invariable.
Its low price makes it accessible
to every small and medium-sized delusion.
Even if you lose a fake, it's still a bargain:
crying for lies comes cheaper.

You resent that so many admirers crowd
against your shop window

καὶ μέσα ψυχὴ νὰ μὴν μπαίνει.

Ἔτσι γίνεται. Ἀπ' ἔξω μόνο στὴ βιτρίνα
θορυβοῦμε οἱ λάτρεις τῆς ἀλήθειας.
Ποιὰ ψυχὴ διαθέτει τὸ μὴ ἀναγραφόμενο
κόστος τῆς ἀπόκτησης.

Ἐξάλλου ἂς μὴν κρυβόμαστε.
Κάθε ἀλήθεια δὲν εἶναι ὅλη χρυσὸς
μήτε ὅλο πολύτιμοι λίθοι.

Δὲν σ' ἀγαπῶ.

Χρυσὴ ἀλήθεια εἶναι αὐτὸ
ἢ οὐράνιο ποὺ σοῦ ἀσπρίζει τὸ αἷμα;
Πολύτιμοι λίθοι εἶναι
ἢ ἄγριος λιθοβολισμός;

Ρίξου λοιπὸν στὰ φὸ μπιζού.

Τί λές, κουτὸς εἶναι ὁ θάνατος
ποὺ προτιμᾶ τὴν ψεύτικη ζωή μας;

and not a living soul comes inside.

So it goes. We truth lovers make noise
only outside, in front of the shop window.
Which soul can afford the unmarked
price of acquisition.

Besides, let's be frank.
Not every truth is solid gold
nor is it all precious stones.

I don't love you.

Is this a golden truth
or uranium blanching your blood?
Are these precious stones
or is this a savage stoning?

So, throw yourself at fashion jewelry.

Do you think Death is stupid
to prefer our fake lives?

ΕΚΤΡΟΠΗ

Ἀντὶ γιὰ ὑακίνθους
εἶπα νὰ σοῦ φέρω σήμερα ἡλιοτρόπια
νὰ ἔχει ἡ φροντίδα μου πιὸ εὐθυτενὲς κοτσάνι
καὶ τὸ ὀστεῶδες πλέον νόημά της νὰ μοῦ φανεῖ
στρογγυλοπρόσωπο ἡλιόσπορους γεμάτο.

Ἡλιοτρόπια. Συσσωρευτὲς λάμπουσας θερμότητας.
Εὐχήθηκα νὰ ἐπωφεληθεῖς.

Κι ἀφοῦ ἐτακτοποίησα σὲ ὕψος ὁμοιόμορφο
αἰσθητικὰ τὸ χρέος μου στὸ βάζο
κοντοστάθηκα λίγο νὰ βεβαιωθῶ
ὅτι τὰ ἡλιοτρόπια θὰ τραποῦν
ἐκεῖ ποὺ ἐπαγγέλλει τὸ ὄνομά τους.

Κατάπληκτη νὰ στρέφουνε τὰ εἶδα
πρὸς τῆς εὐχῆς μου τὴν παράφρονα ἐκπλήρωση
κοιτάζοντας ἀντὶ τὸν ἥλιο ἐσένα.

Τιμῆς ἕνεκεν.
Ὑπῆρξες
χιλιάδες ἔτη φωτὸς
ἀπέχεις.

DEFLECTION

Instead of hyacinths
I thought I'd bring you sunflowers today
so my care would stand on upright stems
and the sense of it, now nothing but bones, would seem to me
round-faced, filled with sunflower seeds.

Sunflowers. Heat accumulators.
I wished you could benefit.

And after I arranged my duty aesthetically
at uniform height in the vase,
I paused a while to assure myself
the sunflowers would turn toward
what their name announces.

Astonished, I saw them deflecting
toward the wild fulfillment of my wish
looking at you instead of the sun.

A tribute.
You have lived
and are thousands of light years
away.

ΜΕΤΑΚΟΜΙΔΗ — ΘΕΟΦΑΝΕΙΑ

Φοβᾶται νὰ σκύψει πιὸ μέσα τὸ φῶς.
Ἂς ρίξει μιά του ἀκτίνα τὸ σουβλερὸ φακό της
νὰ φανεῖ πῶς αἴρουν ἄλλοι τὸ ἁμάρτημα
τῆς ἐκλείψεώς Του.

Ἐστραμμένος ὁ θαυμασμός μου
στὰ κατάλοιπά σου ἀκούει
μὲ τί ἀταραξία περιφρονητικὴ βαθμολογοῦν
τὸν ἀνίερο ἦχο τῆς ἀξίνας
νὰ γκρεμίζει τώρα τὸν ἐγκλεισμό σου
ἐντὸς γαλήνης λένε.

Βλέπω
τοῦ ἐγκλεισμοῦ σου τὰ κατάλοιπα
μὲ τὸ δέος μου ἐστραμμένο στὴν ὑπάκοη
ἐντὸς ἱστοῦ ἀκινησίας διάταξή τους
ὅπως τὰ τοποθέτησε ἀρχικὰ ἡ κίνηση
ὥστε λειτουργικὴ νὰ εἶναι τῆς ὑπάρξεως
ἡ ὁδοιπορία
— ὅταν κουράζεται ὁ νοῦς στὸ μέτωπο
νὰ ἀναπαύεται τὸ χέρι.

Κενά, διάδρομοι ἔρημοι διατρέχουν
τῆς διατάξεως τὴν ὑπακοὴ
μεγάλη σιγὴ ἐκεῖ ποὺ σεργιανοῦσε
ἄλλοτε θορυβώδης τοῦ αἵματος ἡ πολυκοσμία.

•

TRANSPORTATION OF REMAINS—THEOPHANY

The light is afraid to bend over.
Let one ray point its flashlight
to show how others bear the sin
of His eclipse.

Facing your remains,
my admiration listens
for the disdainful composure with which they rate
the sacrilegious sound of the pickax
that now demolishes your confinement
in peace, they say.

I look
at the remains of your confinement
my awe facing their obedient placement
within a web of immobility
just as motion first positioned them
so that the march of existence
would be functional
—whenever the mind grows weary
the hand may rest.

Empty spaces, deserted corridors run through
the obedient placement,
great silence where the blood's noisy
multitudes once took their walks.

•

Ἀπὸ τὸ σήμαντρο
μὲ κωδικὸ τὸ ὡραῖο κεφάλι
λείπει τὸ γλωσσίδι
λείπει καὶ τὸ σκοινὶ ποὺ ἔστελνε
τὶς ἐντολὲς τοῦ ὑψίστου ἐγκεφάλου
στὰ εὐλαβικὰ τοῦ σώματος πλήθη.

Ἄφθαρτο μὲ καθησύχασαν πὼς εἶναι
τὸ μεταλλικὸ κουτὶ ἐντὸς τοῦ ὁποίου
νέο σκότος προοδευτικότερο ἀτάκτως
ἐρριμμένο τὴν περίληψή σου ὑποδέχεται.

Ἄφθαρτη καὶ ἡ γραβάτα σου πιασμένη
στὸ εἴρων ράμφος τῆς ἀξίνας.
Σθεναρὸς ὁ κόμπος της ἐφτασφράγιστο κρατοῦσε
τὸ κλείσιμο τοῦ κύκλου ποὺ ἔτρεξε ὁ λαιμός.

Μέγας θυμὸς θανάτου θιγεὶς μοῦ τὴν ἐπέστρεψε
ὡς ἀντιστασιακὴ ἀπὸ συνθετικὸ μετάξι
ἀκατανίκητο.

Φρίττω. Ἐγὼ ρεγιόν; Τόσο φτηνὰ μὲ τεχνητὸ
μεταξοσκώληκα σὲ στόλισα γιὰ τὸ ἐπισημότερο
ποὺ πήγαινες ἀπὸ ὅλα τὰ σὲ χάνω;

From the bell
whose code was the handsome head
the tongue is missing
missing too is the cord that sent
commandments of the almighty brain
to the body's reverent masses.

Indestructible, they assured me,
the metal box inside of which
a new, more radical disorderly darkness
receives your synopsis.

Indestructible, too, your necktie
caught on the ironic pickax beak.
The robust sevenfold knot was sealing
the circle around which the neck ran.

Death's great wrath, vexed, returned the tie to me
because it proved resistant, made of synthetic silk,
invincible.

I'm appalled. Me, rayon? Dressing you up in cheap
artificial silkworm, for this most formal
of all my losing-yous?

ΥΠΟ ΤΟ ΜΗΔΕΝ

Τρέμεις βροχή.
Σὲ φοβέρισε ὁ μετεωρολόγος
ὅτι θὰ γίνεις αὔριο χιόνι;

Ἐμᾶς νὰ δεῖς
θὰ λιώσετε θὰ λιώσετε προβλέπει.

BELOW ZERO

You're trembling, rain.
Did the weatherman threaten
that tomorrow you'd turn to snow?

Look at us,
you'll melt, he forecasts, you'll melt.

ΕΚΡΗΚΤΙΚΟ ΠΟΡΙΣΜΑ

Κυνηγέ,
ὑποπτεύομαι γιατί σκοτώνεις τὰ πουλιά.
Τὰ ἀπωθημένα σου φτερὰ ἐκδικεῖσαι.

Λυτρώσου.
Ὅλων μας σχεδὸν τὰ πετάγματα
κάποια τὰ βρῆκε ἀζύγιαστη
ἢ ζυγιασμένη σφαίρα.

Εἴτε σκάρτο νερουλὸ ἤτανε τὸ Ἰκάριο
κερὶ
εἴτε γιατὶ ὁ ἥλιος εἶναι συνεργάσιμος
μονάχα μὲ τὴ δύση του
εἴτε γιατὶ κατὰ τὴν ἀπογείωση ἐξερράγη
ἐκρηκτικὸς ἀντίπαλος.

Ὑπολόγισε τώρα τί φτερὰ ταπείνωσε
ἑνὸς κλουβιοῦ τὸ ὕψος ὅτι τάχα
κελαηδοῦσαν γήινα καθημερινὰ
λὲς καὶ ἡ ἀνάγκη ὑπέργεια νὰ κελαηδήσεις
δὲν εἶναι γήινη δὲν εἶναι καθημερινή.

Μνημονεύω χώρια, μὲ εὐλάβεια προσευχετικὴ
τὰ αὐτοκτόνα ἐκεῖνα πετάγματα
μὲ σφαίρα ποὺ κρυφὰ τοὺς ἐπρομήθευσε
τοῦ ἀκατανόητου ἡ μεγάλη γενναιότης
δεδικαίωται:

EXPLOSIVE FINDING

Hunter,
I suspect I know why you kill birds.
You take revenge on your repressed wings.

Take it easy.
Almost everyone's flights
have been hit by either
weighted or nonweighted bullets.

Perhaps because the Icarian wax was defective
watery
or because the sun collaborates
only with its setting
or else because an explosive rival
exploded during takeoff.

Now count how many wings were humbled
by the height of a cage, supposedly because
they sang terrestrially by day
as if to sing super-terrestrially
were not a terrestrial, not a daily need.

With prayerful piety I mention separately
those flights that killed themselves
with bullets secretly supplied
by the great valor of the Inexplicable.
But *he who is dead is freed from sin:*

ἡ νεκροψία ὅλης αὐτῆς τῆς καντεμᾶς
ἔδειξε πὼς τὰ μόνα καλότυχα φτερὰ
τὰ εἶχε ἡ ματαιότης.

Ἠρέμησε λοιπόν.
Ἔχω κι ἐγὼ ἕνα σωρὸ ἀπωθημένους οὐρανοὺς
μὰ δὲ σκοτώνω ἄστρα.

Καὶ ἂν καμιὰ φορὰ ἀπὸ μανία ἀδέσποτη συμβεῖ
κάποιο νὰ σημαδέψω
τὸ πολὺ νὰ κλείσω τὸν τραυματία κελαηδισμό του
σ᾽ ἕνα κλουβάκι στίχου φευγαλέο.

the autopsy performed on all this tough luck
revealed that the only fortunate wings
belonged to vanity.

So calm down.
I myself have lots of repressed skies
but I do not kill stars.

And if sometimes in a stray rage
I take aim at one
the worst I'll do is shut its wounded song
in the small fleeting cage of a verse.

ΜΥΓΔΑΛΙΑΣ ΑΠΟΚΡΙΕΣ

Χαρὰ Θεοῦ στὸ πάρκο
ὡραῖες Ἀλκυονίδες μέρες
ντυμένες πρωινὸ μὲ παραδοσιακὴ
στολὴ ἐκτύφλωσης μοιράζουν δωρεὰν
παιδάκια μπαλόνια παγκάκια
μάσκες Ἀρλεκίνου εὐδιαθεσίας
ἀεράκι καλεῖ σὲ χορὸ σερπαντίνες
περιστέρια λουστράκια γυαλίζουν
μὲ χαρτοπόλεμο τὰ σκονισμένα ράμφη
κουλούρια ντυμένα πειρατὲς μὲ ἕνα μάτι
τενεκεδένια φτερὰ πεταλούδας ἐπάνω
σὲ ἀναπηρικὸ παιχνίδι μὲ ρόδες ποὺ
τὸ τσουλάει ἐφήμερος κρότος ντυμένος
παιδάκια ἡ μικρότερη ἐγγονή μου χανουμάκι
Δούρειος ἵππος τὰ πιὸ μεγάλα ἄλλα μου
μπαλόνια καρφίτσες ντυμένες ρολόγια
σκᾶνε τσὰφ ἐκκωφαντικὰ μπαλόνια
παιδάκια κλάματα ἀτάραχα ἀτάραχα
ἀπόμερα παγκάκια ποὺ λιάζονται
καθήμενα ἁπλανῶς ἐπὶ γερόντων.

THE ALMOND TREE'S CARNIVAL

Glorious sun in the park
beautiful halcyon days
masquerade as morning in traditional
costumes of blindbrightness, hand out free
children balloons benches
masks of harlequin gladness
a breeze invites streamers to dance
shoeshine pigeons polish
dusty beaks with confetti
bread-rings costumed as one-eyed pirates
tin butterfly wings on
wheeled invalid toys pulled by
an ephemeral rattling costumed as
children my youngest granddaughter a little harem girl
my older ones the Trojan Horse
balloons pins costumed as clocks
bursting pop! deafening balloons
children cries impassive impassive
distant benches basking in the sun
seated without expression on the elderly.

ΧΛΟΗ ΘΕΡΜΟΚΗΠΙΟΥ (2005)

GREENHOUSE GRASS (2005)

ΔΙΔΑΚΤΙΚΗ ΥΛΗ

Χρόνε
τὴ διατριβή μου σοῦ ὑποβάλλω
μὲ θέμα της ἐσένα βασικὰ
γιατὶ αὐτὸ ποὺ εἶμαι τώρα
ἐσὺ τὸ ἔφτασες ἐδῶ.

Φτωχοὶ τῆς φύσης μου οἱ πόροι
δὲ μ' ἔστειλε γιὰ ἀνώτερη ἀμάθεια
στὸ ἐξωτερικό. Ἔμεινα ἐδῶ στὸ νοίκι
μιᾶς χαμπλοτάβανης ἐσωτερικῆς
πατριδογνωσίας.

Οἰκονομικὴ
μέθοδο ἄνευ διδασκάλου ἀκολούθησα
καὶ κάθε ἄνευ γενικῶς
ποὺ εἶναι μέθοδος εὐρύτερης μαθήσεως.

Τί τράβηξα δὲ λέγεται ἀδύνατον νὰ μπῶ
στὸ δύσκολο κεφάλαιο
τοῦ «ἄνευ σημασίας».
Ὅ,τι γιὰ μένα εἶχε
ἤτανε ἄνευ γιὰ τοὺς ἄλλους.
Κι ἐνῶ μὲ ἐπιμέλεια ἀπορούσα
τὸ ἀπορώντας μοῦ ἔβαζε μηδέν.
Διόρθωνα τὸ βαθμὸ ἐκ νέου ἀπορώντας
μὲ τὴν ἄνευ λόγου μέθοδό σου
χρόνε

PROGRAM OF STUDY

Time
I submit my thesis to you
with you as its basic subject
since what I am now
arrived here thanks to you.

My nature had no means
to send me abroad for the study of
higher illiteracy. Here I stayed
renting a low-ceilinged
internal history course.

I've followed a cheap
method of study, without a teacher
and every *without* in general
which is a method of broader learning.

What I went through is beyond words, impossible to
reach the difficult chapter
"Without Importance."
Whatever was with for me
was without for others.
And while I studiously wondered
wondering gave me a zero.
I improved my grade by wondering again
about your method
Time

νὰ φέρνεις ἀλλαγὲς καὶ ἐν τῷ ἅμα
νὰ παίρνεις πίσω σβήνοντας ὁλότελα
τὴν προηγούμενη τὴν ἤπια μορφὴ
ποὺ εἴχανε τὰ πράγματα
πρὶν γίνουν σπουδασμένα.

Καὶ τώρα ἀκόμα
μὲ τὴ μέθοδο τοῦ ἄνευ μεγαλώνοντας
σμικρύνομαι σαστίζω ἀπορῶ
πῶς ἄλλαξαν ἀκόμα καὶ τὰ ἄνευ
τόσο συχνὰ δὲν ἦταν

πῶς ἄλλαξε ὁ θάνατος
τόσο συχνὸς δὲν ἦταν

ὅταν ἐνθέρμως μοῦ τὸν σύστησε ἡ ἀγάπη.

to bring changes without reason and right away to
take back, erasing completely
the previous gentle form
things take
before they're learned.

And even now
growing old with the without method
I shrink, get confused, wonder
how even the withouts have changed
they were not so frequent

how death has changed
it was not so frequent

when warmly introduced to me by love.

ΑΝΑΚΙΝΗΣΤΕ ΚΑΛΑ ΠΡΟ ΤΗΣ ΧΡΗΣΕΩΣ

Πρόσωπα ἔργα καὶ ἡμέραι
ὅλα θυελλώδη
ἐνθάδε κεῖνται ἀραγμένα
ὅλα στὴν ἴδια ἀκύμαντη γαλήνη.

Ἄραγε ἀπὸ τί ἐλησμονήθηκαν;

Ἐσωκλείονται ὁδηγίες.
Ἄν τὶς διαβάσεις προσεκτικὰ
Σύνθεση
Προφυλάξεις
Δοσολογία
ἕν κοχλιάριον τοῦ καφὲ καὶ οὔτε φῶς νηστικὸ
ἢ μιὰ μεγάλη ξέχειλη ὡς ἀπάνω
ἐκτυφλωτικὴ ρευστότητα

θὰ δεῖς ὅτι
τὶς ἴδιες θανατηφόρες παρενέργειες ποὺ ἔχει
ἡ μικρὴ δόση ἀγάπης
τὶς ἴδιες ἀκριβῶς ἐπιφυλάσσει καὶ ἡ μεγάλη.

Γι᾽ αὐτὸ καὶ στὸ ἐρώτημα

ἄραγε ἀπὸ τί ἐλησμονήθηκαν

βλέπεις χαραγμένο
τόσο ἀναπάντητο χορτάριασμα.

SHAKE WELL BEFORE USING

Faces, works and days,
tempestuous all,
here lie at anchor,
resting in waveless peace.

For what were they forgotten?

Instructions enclosed.
If you read them carefully—
Description
Warnings
Dosage:
a coffee spoon, if that, of fasting light
or else a great outpouring of
blinding fluidity—

you will see that
the lethal side effects
of a small dose of love
are exactly the same as those of a large one.

That's why the question

for what were they forgotten?

shows you, engraved,
a profusion of unanswered weeds.

Η ΛΙΠΟΤΑΞΙΑ ΤΗΣ ΧΙΟΝΑΤΗΣ

Έτσι
χωρὶς ποτὲ νὰ μοῦ διαβάσεις παραμύθια
ὅπως χωρὶς σὲ μεγαλώσανε καὶ σένα
σπαρτιάτικα — ἐνῶ καλοπερνοῦν τὰ ψέματα
καὶ ψέμα ὅτι τρέφονται μὲ μέλανα ζωμό.
Τρέφονται μὲ ἀνάγκες μας
ἀνώτερες κι ἀπὸ βασιλικὸ πολτό.

Σὲ νυχτωμένο δάσος σὲ ἄφησε ὁ ποιὸς
καὶ σὺ δὲ ρώτησες ποτὲ κανένα παραμύθι
πῶς νὰ διαφύγεις καὶ ἀπὸ ποῦ.
Καὶ μόνο φόβοι
δίνανε στοὺς φόβους σου κουράγιο
ἐκεῖ ἀμετακίνητη νὰ μένεις
στοῦ ἀνέμου τὰ μουγκρίσματα
τὴ νύχτα ὅσο ξέσκιζε τῶν δέντρων τὰ κλαδιὰ
τὰ ὦτα καὶ τὰ χρόνια.

Έτσι ἀκριβῶς μεγάλωσες καὶ μένα,
σπαρτιάτικα, μὲ νυχτωμένου δάσους
τὸν μέλανα ζωμὸ
δὲ μ' ἔστειλες ποτὲ σὲ παραμύθι
νὰ διαφύγω ἀπὸ ποῦ.

Κι ἐγὼ ὅπως ἐσὺ ποτὲ δὲ διανοήθηκα
σπιτάκι φωτισμένο στὸ βάθος νὰ διακρίνω
ποτὲ δὲν μπῆκα στῆς Χιονάτης τὴ δανεικὴ ὁδὸ

SNOW WHITE'S DESERTION

Just like that
without ever reading fairy tales to me
the way you were brought up, without—
the Spartan way—while lies live in luxury
and it's a lie that they're fed black broth.
They feed on our needs
superior even to royal jelly.

Left in a benighted forest by some Who,
you never asked a fairy tale,
how to escape and by which road.
And only fears
encouraged your fears
so you would stand there transfixed
in the roaring wind
that in the night ripped branches off trees
split ears and years.

Exactly how you brought me up too,
the Spartan way, with a benighted forest's
black broth
you never sent me to a fairy tale
through which I could escape.

And like you, I've never imagined myself
spotting a lighted cottage in the distance
I've never walked on Snow White's borrowed road

δὲ χώθηκα ποτὲ σὲ ξένη σούπα
νὰ κοιμηθῶ
οὔτε ξεπαγιασμένη καταβρόχθισα
μικρόσωμο κρεβάτι μὲ νάνους σκεπασμένο
γιὰ νὰ κρατιέται ζεστουλό.

Μάνα, λὲς νὰ εἶναι
κληρονομικὴ ἡ πραγματικότης;

I've never fallen into a stranger's soup
to get some sleep
nor have I devoured frozen stiff
a tiny bed covered with dwarves
who kept it warm and cozy.

Mom, do you believe
reality is hereditary?

ΕΠΩΔΥΝΗ ΑΠΟΚΑΛΥΨΗ

Ὅ,τι λὲς στὴν πένα τὸ γράφει.
Σκέπτεσαι θυμᾶσαι νομίζεις ἀγαπᾶς ὑπαγορεύεις.

Μερικὰ τὰ ἀποσιωπᾶς.
Ὄχι πὼς εἶσαι ὑποκριτὴς ἀλλὰ
λιγάκι σὰ νὰ ντρέπεσαι ποὺ εἶναι τόσο λίγα
καὶ σὰ νὰ κομματιάζεσαι τόσα πολλὰ ποὺ εἶναι.

Μὲ ἀφοσίωση σὲ ἀκοῦνε οἱ λέξεις
σὲ ἀντιγράφουν καὶ ἡ πένα διψασμένη
ρουφάει ὅσο μελάνι ἀφήνουν πίσω τους
—σὰν τὶς σουπιὲς— τὰ συνταρακτικὰ
θολώνει ἡ σύλληψή τους.

Ὅπως σοῦ ὑπαγόρευσε ἡ μοίρα νὰ τὰ ζήσεις
γραμμένα σὲ δικό της ἀπορροφητικὸ χαρτὶ
ἔτσι ἀκριβῶς κι ἐσὺ τὰ ὑπαγορεύεις
στὴν ἄγνωστη ποιότητα τοῦ μέσου ποὺ διαθέτεις.

Καμιὰ φορὰ ὅταν ἡ πένα μπάζει κρύο
γιατὶ οἱ προφυλάξεις ἔχουνε πετσικάρει
ἀπ' τῶν δεινῶν τὴν παλαιότητα
λίγο παραμορφώνεις τὴν εἰκόνα —
αἴσθημα ποὺ δριμὺ χειμώνα δρέπει
τὸ στρέφεις νὰ μαζεύει χαμομήλια
καὶ κάπως ἔτσι γλυκαίνει τοῦ κειμένου ὁ καιρός.

•

PAINFUL REVELATION

Whatever you tell the pen, it writes.
You think remember suppose love dictate.

Some things you pass over in silence.
You're no hypocrite but
you may be ashamed they're so few
or you may go to pieces they're so many.

Words listen to you with devotion
they copy you and the thirsty pen
imbibes all the ink that stupefying facts
—like cuttlefish—leave in their wake,
their perception blurs.

Just as fate dictated life instructions to you
as they were written on its own blotting paper
so you dictate them
to the unknown quality of the medium at your disposal.

Sometimes when the pen lets the cold in
because precautions warp
due to the age of the hardships,
you distort the image slightly—
turning a feeling that reaps bitter winter
into one that plucks chamomiles
and so the text's weather grows milder.

•

Ὅλα ἐτοῦτα καὶ ἄλλα μαζὶ
τὰ παίρνει φεύγοντας ὁ χρόνος
σὰ νά 'τανε δικά του.
Κάποια στιγμὴ τοῦ τὰ ζητᾶς τ' ἀνοίγεις
θέλεις νὰ δεῖς ἐὰν θυμᾶται τὸ χαρτὶ ὅσα
τοῦ ὑπαγόρευσες γιατὶ ἀκόμα
καὶ τῆς ἄψυχης ἐγγύησης ἡ μνήμη
μὲ τὸν καιρὸ κι αὐτὴ ἀδυνατίζει.

Ταράζεσαι χλωμιάζεις βλέπεις
νά 'χουν γραφτεῖ πράγματα ποὺ δὲν εἶπες
τὸν ἑαυτό σου ἀγνώριστο
κι οἱ πράξεις του θρασύδειλες
νὰ ἐνοχοποιοῦν ἄλλων τὴν προδοσία
ἐνῶ ἡ δική σου σὲ ἀνύψωση
νὰ θριαμβεύει ὡς θύμα

κι ἄλλα κι ἄλλα τερατώδη, ἐπονείδιστα
ποὺ καὶ νεκρὸς νὰ εἶσαι
ντρέπεσαι νὰ τὰ πεῖς
μὲ τὸ γυμνὸ ὄνομά τους.

Φρίττεις κι ἑρμηνεύεις
πὼς ὅλα εἶναι βγαλμένα
τάχα ἀπ' τῆς γραφῆς τὸ ἄρρωστο μυαλό.

Σὲ λιγοστεύει σὲ ταπεινώνει νὰ παραδεχτεῖς
πὼς ὅλ' αὐτὰ τὰ ἀνίδεα ποὺ γράφουμε

Upon leaving, time
takes all these things and more with it
as if they were its own.
One day you ask for their return, you open them
you want to see if the paper remembers everything
you've dictated because
even the memory of an inanimate guarantee
gradually grows dim.

You get upset turn pale see
things written down you haven't said
your own self unrecognizable,
its swaggering boasts
incriminate the betrayal of others
while yours, glorified,
triumph as victim

these and many more things, monstrous, ignominious,
which, even if you're dead
you're ashamed to call
by their naked names.

Horrified, you interpret them all
as if they were the product of
writing's diseased mind.

It humbles, humiliates you to admit
that all the ignorant things we write

γνωρίζουνε γιὰ μᾶς περισσότερα
καὶ πιὸ ἀβυσσαλέα
ἀπ᾽ ὅσα μισοξέρουν ὅσα ζήσαμε.

know more
and more abysmally about us
than all the things we've lived only half-know.

ΑΣΚΗΣΕΙΣ ΓΙΑ ΝΑ ΧΑΣΕΤΕ ΤΑ ΠΕΡΙΤΤΑ
ΚΙΛΑ ΣΕ ΣΥΝΤΟΜΟ ΧΡΟΝΙΚΟ ΔΙΑΣΤΗΜΑ

Ξαπλῶστε. Ἐπάνω σὲ κάτι σκληρό.
Στὴν ἀρχὴ πονᾶνε ἴσως τῶν ἀνέσεων οἱ σπόνδυλοι
ἀλλὰ σιγὰ σιγὰ ἀνώδυνα ἰσιώνει κυπαρίσσι
τῆς ἀκινησίας ἡ πλάτη.

Συμπτύξτε τώρα τὶς κακιὲς συνήθειές σας
σὲ ἄκαμπτη εὐθεία.
Φέρτε στὸ στῆθος χαλαρὰ τὰ χέρια
σὰν πρόχειρες φτερούγες προσωρινῶν ἀγγέλων.
Μὴν ἀλλάζετε στάση.
Τὸ ἀνάσκελα κωπηλατεῖ ἐπιδέξια.

Μὴ φοβάστε. Ὁ φόβος παχαίνει
περιέχει πείνα.
Μὴ μασουλᾶτε αἰσθήσεις. Πολλὲς θερμίδες.
Σ᾽ αὐτὲς ὀφείλεται τὸ πάχος τῶν στερήσεων.

Τὰ ματάκια κλειστὰ παρακαλῶ τελείως
ὄχι χαραμάδες παρεξηγήσιμες
ὄχι γλειφιτζούρια φωτός.
Ἐκπέμπουν ὑπεριώδη νοσταλγία.

Ἐκπνεῦστε μὲ δύναμη, ἀκίνητοι
μὴν ἀναπνέετε μὴν ἀναπνέετε
κινδυνεύει νὰ φανεῖ στὴν ἀκτινογραφία
ὁ μισὸς βαρκάρης μόνο.

•

EXERCISES FOR WEIGHT LOSS
IN NO TIME AT ALL

Lie down. On something hard.
At first your leisure vertebrae may hurt
but gradually, painlessly, immobility
straightens its back till it stands there like a cypress.

Now compress your bad habits
into one rigid line.
Rest your hands on your chest
like the makeshift wings of a provisional angel.
Do not shift position.
The supine rows best.

Don't be afraid. Fear makes you fat,
it contains hunger.
Don't chew on sensations. Too many calories.
They cause the fat of deprivations.

Close your eyes, please
no dubious chinks
no lollipops of light.
They emit ultraviolet nostalgia.

Fully exhale, hold still
don't breathe, don't breathe
lest only half the ferryman
appear on the X-ray.

•

Ἀφεθεῖτε τώρα στὴν τσουλήθρα τοῦ ὕπνου.
Θὰ σᾶς βάλω σὲ κασέτα, χαλαρῶστε,
τὸ νανούρισμα τῆς μάνας σας
νάνι νάνι τὸ μωράκι μου
θέλοντας καὶ μὴ θὰ κάνει.

Ζυγιστεῖτε. Ἀκίνητοι παρακαλῶ
στὸ σῶμα σας ὑπάρχει ἔνθετη ζυγαριά.

Let yourself slide down sleep.
You just relax, I'll play
your mother's lullaby on tape
hush little baby hush
like it or not I say.

Weigh yourself. Please hold still:
nested inside your body a scale awaits.

ΕΠΙΣΚΕΥΑΣΤΙΚΑ ΔΑΝΕΙΑ

Ἐκκλησάκι ἔρημο ἐγκαταλειμμένο πιστευτό.
Θαρρεῖς ὅτι τὸ ἔχτισε ἐρείπωση.
Τὰ κεραμίδια στὸν τροῦλο
τρύπιο σάλι ριγμένο
στὴ γηραιὰ καμπούρα τῆς ἀνάτασης.
Τὰ μικρὰ παράθυρα κρέμονται
κάπως στραβὰ στὸν τοῖχο
σὰν εἰκονίτσες ποὺ σεισμὸς τὶς μετακίνησε
ἀπὸ τῆς πίστης τὸ ἴσιο.
Βιτρὸ στὰ τζάμια συνθεμένα
μὲ πολυκαιρινῆς βροχῆς σταγόνες ραγισμένες.

Ἄραγε νὰ ζεῖ μέσα ἡ ἁγιότης
τρεφόμενη μὲ σβηστὰ κεράκια μόνο;

Κλειδωμένη ἡ ἀμφίβια πόρτα
— καὶ στὸ μέσα σκότος βυθισμένη ζεῖ
καὶ στὸ φῶς ἔξω κολυμπάει.
Ἐπάνω της τὴν πλάτη του ἀκουμπώντας
ἕνα σκαλοπατάκι
ζητιανεύει λίγην ἐπισκευή. Ἔχει σπάσει.

Καὶ ἡ φύση ποὺ ὅλα τὰ καλοπιάνει
καὶ τὴν ἀκμὴ λατρεύει
καὶ στὴ φθορὰ χατίρι δὲ χαλάει

ἐπισκευάζει τὴ ρωγμὴ στὸ σκαλοπάτι

REPAIR LOANS

A desolate derelict credible chapel.
You'd think ruin itself had built it.
The dome's tiles
a moth-eaten shawl thrown over
exaltation's old hunchback.
The narrow windows hang
somewhat crooked on the wall
like icons an earthquake shifted
from belief's rectitude.
Stained-glass windowpanes made
from cracked drops of antique rain.

Could it be that sanctity lives inside
fed solely on small extinguished candles?

The locked door, amphibious—
living sunk in interior darkness
and swimming in exterior light.
Leaning its back against it,
a tiny step
begs to be repaired. It's broken.

And nature, which flatters all—
adoring zeniths
and giving in to decay's whims—

repairs the crack in the step

πολύχρωμα γεμίζοντάς την
μὲ τσουκνίδες γαϊδουράγκαθα μολόχες
δαφνόφυλλα καὶ πικροπαπαροῦνες.

Καὶ γίνεται αἴφνης ἀνοιξιάτικος
εὐδιάθετος γραφικὸς αἰσιόδοξος ὁ τρόμος
γιὰ τὴν ἐρείπωση τῆς ἐγκατάλειψής μας.

filling it in colorfully
with nettles thistles mallows
bay leaves and bitter poppies.

And suddenly the terror
of our abandonment's ruin turns springlike
cheerful optimistic picturesque.

ΑΝΕΝΔΟΤΗ

Ὅλοι οἱ καλεσμένοι τοῦ ὀνείρου
εἶχαν λογικὰ ντυθεῖ
καθεὶς μὲ τὴ σκιά του
κι ἀνάριχτη μιὰ λασπωμένη κάπα
ποὺ ὕφανε τὸ θέλημα
στὸν πρῶτο πρῶτο ἀργαλειὸ τοῦ πεπρωμένου.

Μόνο ἐσὺ πατέρα μου ἤσουν παραφωνία.
Λευκὸ ἀπληροφόρητο κουστούμι
ὁλομέταξο φοροῦσες
τὸ παντελόνι ἔτριζε μέσα στὸ ἄφθαρτό του
ἡ τσάκιση ἀπτόητη ὁλόρθη
σὰ νὰ μὴν ἦταν χρόνια ξαπλωμένη.

Τρελάθηκες σοῦ φώναξα
κουστούμι καλοκαιρινὸ μέσα στὸ καταχείμωνο;
Θὲς νὰ παγώσεις κι ἄλλο;

Εἰς ὑγείαν εἶπες μὴν ἀνησυχεῖς
ὁ καιρὸς ἐδῶ εἶναι ἀδιάφορος... ἀδιάφορος...
κι ἄδειασες μονορούφι μαῦρο πάτο
τὸ πλῆρες σκόρπισμά σου

ἀδιάφορος... ἀδιάφορος... ἀδιάφορος...

Πολὺ γνωστή μου λέξη.
Κάποτε τὴν ἱκέτευα.

IMPLACABLE

All the guests in the dream
were sensibly dressed
each in his own shadow
and a muddy cloak tossed over the shoulder
woven by will
on destiny's very first loom.

You alone father were out of tune.
Wearing an ignorant
suit of white silk
the trousers grinding in their indestructibility
their standing crease intrepid
as if it hadn't lain flat for years.

You're crazy I screamed
a summer suit in the middle of winter?
Do you want to freeze even more?

To your health you said, don't worry
the weather here is indifferent . . . indifferent . . .
gulping down your own total scattering
to the black dregs

indifferent . . . indifferent . . . indifferent

A most familiar word.
At one time I implored it.

ΜΕΤΑΦΕΡΘΗΚΑΜΕ ΠΑΡΑΠΛΕΥΡΩΣ

(2007)

WE'VE MOVED NEXT DOOR (2007)

Η ΕΠΙΛΕΚΤΙΚΗ ΑΙΩΝΙΟΤΗΣ

«Πίστεψέ με θὰ σ' ἀγαπῶ αἰώνια»
ἐπαναλαμβάνει κάθε λεπτὸ ὁ θάνατος
στὴν αἰωνιότητα

καὶ κείνη βογκώντας
ἀπὸ δυστυχισμένη βεβαιότητα

ἂχ γιατί νὰ μὴν εἶσαι ψεύτης

τὸν καταριέται.

SELECTIVE ETERNITY

"Believe me, I'll love you eternally"
Death repeats every moment
to Eternity

and moaning
with miserable certainty

"oh, can't you just lie for once!"

she curses him.

ΟΥΚ ΟΙΔΑ

Ἐπειδὴ συναναστρέφεσαι
ὕποπτους κόσμους
αὐτὸν ἰδίως τῆς ψυχῆς
κάποια στιγμὴ θὰ σὲ καλέσουν στὴ Δίωξη
γιὰ ἀνακρίσεις γιὰ ἀναγνώριση.

Πρόσεχε
μὲ λακωνικότητα
θὰ ὁμολογήσεις.

Σκοτεινὰ θὰ σὲ ὁδηγήσουν
σὲ καταδότρια αἴθουσα περίκλειστη.
Θὰ καθίσεις
σὲ κάποιο τραπεζάκι γρονθοκοπημένο
μπροστὰ σ' ἕνα ντοσιὲ παχὺ γεμάτο
φωτογραφίες ὑπόπτων.

Θὰ τοὺς ξεφυλλίζουν ἀργὰ ἕναν ἕναν
δὲ θὰ μιλᾶς, θὰ προχωροῦν.
Καὶ μόλις δεῖς τὸ δάχτυλό τους
σὰν κάννη περιστρόφου κολλημένο
ἐπίμονα
στὸν κρόταφο τοῦ ὕποπτου

ἔσο ἕτοιμος θὰ πεῖς

οὐκ οἶδα τὸν ἄνθρωπο

•

I DO NOT KNOW

Because you associate
with suspect worlds
—especially that of the soul—
someday you'll be summoned by the police
for interrogation, identification.

Be careful
your confession
must be terse.

They'll darkly lead you
to a closed-in denouncing room.
You'll sit
at some beat-up table
before a thick file filled
with photographs of suspects.

They'll leaf through them slowly one by one
you'll say nothing, they'll go on.
And as soon as you see their finger
persistently fixed
like the barrel of a revolver
on the suspect's temple

be prepared to say

I do not know the man

•

(τρὶς)

θὰ μετακινεῖται βραδέως ἡ κάννη
θὰ σταθεῖ στὸν κρόταφο τοῦ χρόνου
ἐσὺ ἐκεῖ, σταθερὰ θὰ ἐπιμείνεις

οὐκ οἶδα τὸν ἄνθρωπο

(τρὶς)

ἐξίσου σθεναρὶ ἂν καὶ τρομαγμένη
πρέπει νὰ σταθεῖ ἡ ἀπάντησή σου
μπροστὰ στὴ φωτογραφία τοῦ θανάτου

οὐκ οἶδα τὸν ἄνθρωπο

(τρὶς)

κι ὅταν ἐκνευρισμένη πιὰ ἡ Δίωξη
γρονθοκοπώντας σε
βάναυσα τὸ μοῦτρο σου κολλήσει
ἐπάνω σ' ἕνα ἐξαίσιο ἀχνὸ
σκίτσο μὲ κάρβουνο ὀνείρου

δὲν τὸ ξαναεῖδα

ἅπαξ

θὰ πεῖς.

(thrice)

the barrel will move slowly
then come to a standstill on time's temple
but you'll steadily keep insisting

I do not know the man

(thrice)

equally vigorous though scared
your answer must stand
before death's photo

I do not know the man

(thrice)

and when the police, finally exasperated,
beating you
brutally, thrust your face
on a sublime pale
charcoal sketch of a dream

I never saw it

(once)

      you'll say.

ΜΕΤΑΦΕΡΘΗΚΑΜΕ ΠΑΡΑΠΛΕΥΡΩΣ

Μετὰ τὴν ἀπόφαση
—τίνος;—
νὰ μεταφερθεῖ παραπλεύρως
στὴν ἰσόγεια μνήμη τοῦ θανάτου
τὸ ὄνομά σου

σείστηκε τὸ διατηρητέο νόημα
τοῦ παλιοῦ σπιτιοῦ

σὰ χαλασμένο δόντι ἕτοιμο νὰ πέσει
κουνιόντουσαν οἱ τοῖχοι

ἄδειαζαν τὰ κάδρα
ἕνας πανικὸς μαδοῦσε
τὰ ἀνοιξιάτικα τοπία
ψυχραιμία παρακαλῶ ψυχραιμία
συμβούλευε ἡ νεκρή τους φύση

ἐκκενῶστε τὸ ταβάνι, βυθίζεται
εἰδοποιοῦσα τὶς ἀπλανεῖς μας ἐκεῖ πάνω
ἀναχωρήσεις

καὶ μεταφερθήκαμε παραπλεύρως

ἀκριβῶς
δυὸ τρία σπίτια παρὰ κεῖ
πολὺ κοντὰ

•

WE'VE MOVED NEXT DOOR

After the decision
—whose?—
to move your name next door
to death's
ground-floor memory

the landmarked meaning
of the old house began to shake

like rotten teeth ready to fall
the walls were moving

picture frames emptied
as panic plucked out
the spring landscapes
stay calm please stay calm
their still lives advised

evacuate the ceiling, it's sinking
I warned our fixed
departures up there

and we moved next door

just
two or three houses down the road
very close by
•

πιὸ μακριὰ ὁ ἄνθρωπος
ἀπὸ αὐτὸ ποὺ φτιάχτηκε
δὲν πάει

κι ἔτσι δὲν ἀπομακρύνθηκα
κάθε πρωὶ νὰ βλέπω

τῆς βυσσινὶ ρόμπας σου
τὸ λιωμένο χέρι
ν' ἀνοίγει τῆς συνήθειας τὸ παλιὸ παράθυρο

κι ὅλο κάθε πρωὶ νὰ λέω: ἔλιωσε πάει
νὰ θυμηθῶ αὔριο ἐξάπαντος

κάθε πρωὶ τὸ ἴδιο λιωμένο χέρι
τῆς ρόμπας σου

κι ὅλο ἀρνοῦμαι, ἀναβάλλω
νὰ ἀντικαταστήσω
αὐτὴ τὴν παλιὰ ἐφθαρμένη ὀδύνη
μὲ μιὰ καινούργια

βλέπεις τόσο μόνο, ἕως παραπλεύρως
λίγο πρὶν τὴν ἀλήθεια.
Πιὸ πέρα
δειλιάζει ὁ ἄνθρωπος δὲ μεταφέρεται.

we won't go
farther than what
we're made for

so I didn't distance myself
and every morning I can see

your crimson robe's
frayed hand
opening habit's old window

and every morning I repeat, "it's nothing but threads"
—must remind myself tomorrow without fail—

every morning the same frayed hand
of your robe

and always I refuse and postpone
replacing
this old threadbare sorrow
with a new one

we can see only so far, as far as next door
just up to truth.
Beyond that
we shrink back, cannot be moved.

ΤΟ ΠΡΟΒΛΗΜΑ ΤΗΣ ΣΤΕΓΗΣ

Κύριε
μὴ μᾶς πάρεις κι ἄλλο
τὶς ἀπώλειές μας.

Δὲν ἔχουμε ποῦ ἀλλοῦ νὰ μείνουμε.

THE PROBLEM OF THE ROOF

Lord
don't keep depriving us
of our losses.

We have nowhere else to stay.

ΑΤΙΤΛΟ

Βρέχει μὲ ἀπόλυτη εἰλικρίνεια.
Ἄρα δὲν εἶναι φήμη ὁ οὐρανὸς
ὑπάρχει
καὶ δὲν εἶναι τὸ χῶμα λοιπὸν
ἡ μόνη λύση
ὅπως ἰσχυρίζεται ὁ κάθε τεμπέλης νεκρός.

UNTITLED

It rains with absolute candor.
So the sky is not a rumor
it does exist
and therefore earth is not
the sole solution
as each lazy dead person pretends.

ΠΡΟΣΕΧΕ

Ὅταν στρώνεις τὸ τραπέζι
πρὶν καθίσεις
νὰ ἐλέγχεις σχολαστικὰ
τὴν ἀντικρινή σου καρέκλα

ἂν εἶναι γερὴ μήπως τρίζει
μήπως χαλάρωσαν οἱ ἐγκοπὲς
μήπως φαγώθηκαν οἱ ἁρμοὶ
ἂν ὑποσκάπτει τὸ σκελετὸ
σκουλήκι

γιατὶ ἐκεῖνος ποὺ δὲν κάθεται
γίνεται κάθε μέρα ὅλο καὶ πιὸ βαρύς.

BE CAREFUL

When you set the table
before you take your seat
be sure thoroughly to check
the chair opposite your own

whether it's solid or it creaks
if its notches have loosened
if its joints have been gnawed
whether its frame is undermined by some
worm

for he who does not take his seat
grows heavier by the day.

ΚΑΜΙΑ ΣΧΕΣΗ

Κλαδεύουνε τὰ δέντρα προετοιμαστικὰ
ὥστε ν' ἀνέβει εὐχερῶς ἡ ἄνοιξη σὲ λίγο
ἀνεβάζοντας ἐκ νέου
ἀκμαία τὴ μορφή τους μὲ ἀναλλοίωτο
τὸ σαρκῶδες περσινό της καταπράσινο
σὰ νὰ μὴν κιτρίνισε ποτὲ

—καμία σχέση δηλαδὴ
μὲ κεῖνο τὸ πριονωτὸ ἀνεπίστρεπτο
ποὺ κλαδεύει ἐμᾶς—

τί ἔλεγα, ναί, στὰ πεζοδρόμια
ἔνθεν κακεῖθεν τοῦ δρόμου στοῖβες
φύλλα πρασινοκίτρινα καὶ κλάρες
ὑγρὲς ἀκόμα στάζοντας δακρυσμένες
ἀκριβῶς στὸ σημεῖο
τοῦ ἀποχωρισμοῦ τους ἀπὸ τὰ δέντρα.
Προσωρινά. Κι ὅμως δακρυσμένες.

Φαντάσου τώρα, τί αἰσθάνεται
ἡ ὁριστικότης.

NO RELATION

Trees are pruned in preparation
for spring's quick and easy rise
once again raising
robust figures
with last year's fleshy green unchanged
as if it had never yellowed

—no relation, in other words,
to that serrated *irrevocable*
that prunes us—

what was I saying, yes, on the walks
on both sides of the road, stacks
of yellow-green leaves and branches
still moist, dripping with tears
on the exact spots
of their separation from the trees.
Temporarily. Nevertheless in tears.

Imagine now
how definiteness must feel.

ΠΑΝΣΕΛΗΝΟΣ

Τὸ πρωὶ
ἐκτάκτως σύννεφα τοῦ Αὐγούστου μερικὰ
πέρα στὸ βάθος τοῦ ὁρίζοντα ποὺ τρέμει
σὰ νὰ τὸν διατρέχουν
ρίγη μολυβιὰ

καὶ τὸ βράδυ
ψύχραιμη λιτανεία πανσελήνου
μὲς στὰ στενὰ καὶ ἀδιέξοδα σοκάκια
μιᾶς κάρτας σου ποὺ ἔλαβα
«...κουράστηκα
...λυπᾶμαι. Χαιρετῶ»

μὲ κούριερ ἐντὸς τῆς σήμερον ἐπίδοση.

Τί βιαστικὸς
λὲς καὶ χωρὶς πανσέληνο αὔριο
δὲ θά 'βλεπες νὰ ἐκλείψω.

FULL MOON

In the morning
extraordinarily some August clouds
deep in the horizon trembling
as if leaden-hued shudders
ran through it

and in the evening
the calm procession of a full moon
down the narrow dead-end lanes
of the postcard I received from you
". . . I'm done
. . . sorry. Good-bye"

by courier *same day delivery.*

Such a hurry
as if tomorrow, without a full moon,
you wouldn't see my eclipse.

ΘΑ ΒΓΕΙ ΝΑ ΣΕ ΜΑΛΩΣΕΙ

Λίγο πολὺ ὅλες οἱ λέξεις
φέρνουν καὶ διώχνουν κόσμο
ἀθωώνουν ἢ καταδικάζουν
λίγο πολὺ ὅλες μᾶς ὁδηγοῦν
μὲ κάποιαν ἔκλαμψη κοντὰ στὸ νόημά τους.

Ἀλλὰ τὴ λέξη φεγγάρι
κανένα φῶς δὲν τὴ φτάνει.

Δὲν ἐννοῶ ἐκεῖνο ποὺ ἐκπέμπει
ὅταν διακινεῖ πετρῶδες ἀσήμι.
Γιὰ τὴ λέξη μιλῶ ποὺ καὶ χωρὶς φορτίο
ἀδειανὴ
ἀκόμα καὶ ὡς ἁπλὴ νυχτοφύλαξ
τοῦ λεξιλογίου
ἢ καὶ ὡς δραπέτης ἀπὸ ἔκλειψη ὁλικὴ

πάλι γεμάτη εἶναι
ἀπὸ δική της αὐθεντικὴ ἐπιρροὴ
δική της θαυματουργία.

Κάθε ποὺ τῆς γλώσσας μου τὰ χείλη
βρίσκονται σὲ ζοφερὴ θέση
μόλις τὴν προφέρουν μὲ ἄκρα ταπεινότητα

ἀμέσως προβάλλει
διαχέεται τιμᾶ καταξιώνει

•

IT WILL COME OUT TO SCOLD YOU

All words more or less
draw people near or chase them away
acquit or condemn
all words lead us more or less
by some illumination close to their meaning.

But no light can touch
the word *moonbeam*.

I don't mean what radiates
when it traffics in ores of silver.
I'm talking about the word that—even without cargo
empty
even as vocabulary's
simple night-watchman
or as a runaway from total eclipse—

is again filled
by its own real influence
its own magic.

Every time my tongue's lips
find themselves in a murky spot
as soon as they say it with extreme humility

out it comes
glowing honoring validating—

•

καμιὰ ἄλλη λέξη δὲν ἔδωσε ποτὲ
τέτοιο οὐράνιο λάμπον κύρος
στὸν σκοτεινό, ἄσημο
τοῦ οὐρανίσκου μου θόλο.

Κι ὄχι μόνο.

Κάθε ποὺ τῆς γλώσσας μου τὰ χείλη
ἀτιμάζονται διωγμένα
ἀπὸ τὸ θεοσκότεινο ἀντίο

ἀμέσως προβάλλει ἡ λέξη φεγγάρι
μὲ λαμπερὴ παρρησία
μ' ἕνα φῶς δριμὺ θυμωμένο
καὶ μαλώνει

τί μαλώνει, πές το ἄφοβα

φτύνει κατάμουτρα
τὸ θεοσκότεινο ἀντίο.

no other word has ever given
such luminous celestial prestige
to the dark obscure
vault that is my palate.

And that's not all.

Every time my tongue's lips
are disgraced, chased away
by a pitch-black good-bye

out comes the word *moonbeam*
with brilliant candor
with a bitter angry light
to scold

not to scold—don't be afraid to say the word—

to *spit* in the face
of the pitch-black good-bye.

ΕΠΙΤΥΜΒΙΟ

«Κάθε φιλὶ ποὺ δίνεται, μὰ κάθε ἀνεξαιρέτως
ἕνα τοῖς ἑκατὸ ἀποτελεῖται
ἀπὸ αἰωνιότητα
κι ὅλο τὸ ἄλλο ἀπὸ τὸν κίνδυνο
νά 'ναι τὸ τελευταῖο.»

Ἀλλὰ καὶ τελευταῖο
ἀκόμα πιὸ φιλὶ θὰ λέγεται

ὅσο καιρὸ τουλάχιστον
θὰ τὸ τραβολογᾶνε
ἡ μνήμη ἀπὸ τὴ μιὰ μεριὰ
ἡ λήθη ἀπὸ τὴν ἄλλη
ἡ καθεμιὰ δικό της θεωρώντας το

ὥσπου ὁ δίκαιος Σολομὼν
γιὰ νὰ φανεῖ ποιανῆς δικό της εἶναι
στὴ μέση θ' ἀπειλήσει νὰ τὸ κόψει
μισὸ νὰ πάρει ἡ μιὰ μισὸ ἡ ἄλλη

κι ὅποια ἀπ' τὶς δυὸ κάθε φορὰ
—ποτὲ δὲν εἶναι ἡ ἴδια—
οὐρλιάξει μή.

Κάθε φιλὶ
ἀποτελεῖται ἐξολοκλήρου ἀπὸ τὸν κίνδυνο
νά 'ναι τὸ τελευταῖο.

•

EPITAPH

"One percent of every kiss given,
each one without exception, consists
of eternity
and all the rest the risk
it may be the last."

Even if it's the last
it will be called a kiss all the more

at least as long
as memory on one hand
and oblivion on the other
pull it about
each claiming it for its own

until Solomon the just
to reveal whose it is
threatens to divide it
giving half to one, half to the other

and every time one of the two
—never the same one—
screams "don't."

Every kiss
consists entirely of the risk
it may be the last.

•

Διαρκὲς εἶναι μόνο
ἐκεῖνο τὸ φιλὶ ποὺ οὐδέποτε ἐδόθη.
Σοφές, εἰρηνικὰ τὸ νέμονται
ἡ ἀναμονὴ καὶ ἡ παραίτηση

ἄνθη ἀντίπαλα οἱ δυό τους
σὲ κοινὸ συμβιβασμένο ἀνθοδοχεῖο
κενοτάφιο στολίζουν.

Only the kiss never given
remains everlasting.
Wisely, peacefully it's shared
by expectation and renunciation,

two rival flowers
in one resigned vase
adorning a cenotaph.

ΜΙΣΟ ΦΕΓΓΑΡΙ

Βλέπω ἕνα γούβωμα βαθύ.
Ποιὸ χέρι ἁρπακτικὸ
μπῆκε πῆρε πολὺ ἔφυγε
καὶ δὲν πρόφτασα;

Ἄραγε σὲ ποιὸ ὄνειρο ἀνέθεσα
τοῦ ὅλου τὴ φύλαξη
καὶ τὸ πῆρε ὁ ὕπνος;

Ἀκούω τὸ νυχτολούλουδο
σὰν κοῦκος ρολογιοῦ
πετάγεται ἔξω ἀπ᾽ τὸ ἄρωμά του
φωνάζοντας
νύχτωσε βγὲς νὰ δεῖς

καὶ εἶδα νὰ χαράζεται ψηλὰ

ἕνα μισὸ καὶ οὔτε φεγγάρι

σὰ μαχαιριὰ σὲ ὑπερφυσικὸ θεοῦ σαγόνι

ἢ μᾶλλον σὰν φιλιοῦ τὸ κάτω χεῖλος
καὶ τὸ ἐπάνω νὰ φιλάει τὸ σκοτάδι

— ποιὸς καὶ σὲ ποιὸν μισοεῖπε:
ἂν εἶναι ἀργὰ κοιμήσου στὸ κρεβάτι μου ἐσὺ
κι ἐγὼ στὸν καναπέ.

•

HALF MOON

I see a deep hollow.
Which rapacious hand
walked in took a lot left
and I wasn't there in time?

To which dream did I entrust
the safeguarding of the whole
but the dream fell asleep?

I hear the night flower
leap out of its scent
like the cuckoo from its clock
crying
night is falling come and see

and I saw etched high in the sky

not quite half a moon

like the slash of a knife in a god's supernatural chin

or rather like the lower lip of a kiss
whose upper kisses darkness

—I wonder who half-said to whom
"if it gets late, you take my bed
and I'll sleep on the sofa"

•

Ἄχ, ὑπομνηστικὸ φεγγάρι
στέκεις ἐκεῖ πάνω σὰ μισὴ ὡραιότητα
καὶ σὰν ὁλόκληρη εὐκαιρία
κοιτάζοντάς σε νὰ μετρῶ

πόσα μισὰ δὲν πρόλαβα ν' ἀφήσω.

Ah, memorandum moon
you stand up there like half beauty
and like whole opportunity
I look at you to count

how many halves I had no time to leave.

TA EYPETPA (2010)

THE FINDER'S REWARD (2010)

ΤΑ ΕΥΡΕΤΡΑ

Τὰ ξεφύλλιζες, κοντοστεκόσουν κάθε τόσο
διάβαζες τάχα κάτι σὲ διαπερνοῦσε
ἀδιάβαστες κρυφογελοῦσαν οἱ σελίδες

μετὰ τὰ ζύγιασες ὅλα στὴ χούφτα σου
σὰ νὰ ἦταν κέρματα
χοντρικὰ τὰ ἐξετίμησες
οὐκ ὀλίγα εἶπες
ἔκπληκτος πῶς τ' ἀπέκτησες μὲ ρωτᾶς.

Ὑποκριτή, γραμμὴ δὲ διάβασες
ἀλλιῶς θὰ τό 'βλεπες
τὸ γράφω ἐδῶ μέσα πρῶτο πρῶτο

τὰ εὕρετρα εἶναι
ἐσὺ μοῦ τὰ ἔδωσες
ἐπειδὴ σὲ βρῆκα

σὲ μέτρησα καὶ ἤσουνα πολλὰ
ξαναμετρῶ κι ἤσουν ἀλλιῶς
τὸ ἄφησα νὰ εἶσαι κι ἀπ' τὰ δύο
δὲ σοῦ ἀφαίρεσα οὔτε μία
ἀπ' τὶς χιλιάδες ὡραιότητες ποὺ εἶχες
οὔτε μισὴ ἀπ' τὶς πολύτιμες ἀσκήμιες σου
κόσμε.

THE FINDER'S REWARD

Thumbing through, you hesitated now and then
in your reading, as if something had got to you,
unread, the pages were secretly laughing

then you weighed them all in the palm of your hand
as if they were coins
and made a rough estimate
not so few, you said,
surprised, how did you come by them, you asked me.

Hypocrite, you haven't read a single line
or else you would have seen
it's the first thing I wrote

they're the finder's reward
you gave them to me
because I found you

I took a count and you were numerous
I count again and you were otherwise
I allowed you to be both one and the other
I didn't subtract a single one
of the thousand beauties you possessed
nor one speck of your precious ugliness
World.

Η ΘΡΑΣΕΙΑ ΛΟΓΟΚΛΟΠΟΣ

Τελικὰ
ἀπ᾽ τὸν ἀσίγαστο ἐμφύλιο πόλεμο
μεταξὺ τοῦ ὑπάρχω καὶ τοῦ παύω
τοῦ μιλῶ καὶ τοῦ σώπασα

ἡ μόνη κερδισμένη εἶναι
ἡ διάσημη ἐκείνη πολεμικὴ ἀνταποκρίτρια

ἡ γραφή.

Θρασύτατη λογοκλόπος ἀνίερη

ἀντιγράφει
καὶ τὸ μιλῶ καὶ τὸ σώπασα νὰ ὑπάρχω
ἐπιδέξια παραποιημένο σὲ
διαρκῶ

στοῦ χαρτιοῦ τὸ ἐχέμυθο αὐτί.

THE BRAZEN PLAGIARIST

Of the unremitting civil war
between existing and ceasing to
between speaking and ceasing to
finally

the only winner is
that famous war correspondent

writing.

A brazen unholy plagiarist

it copies
both speaking and ceasing to exist
expertly forged as
lasting

in the paper's closemouthed ear.

ΟΥΣΙΩΔΗΣ ΔΙΑΦΟΡΑ

Τὴ στάχτη κατὰ βάθος δὲν τὴ συμπαθῶ

εἶναι ἀπόλυτη
τὸ ὕφος της δηλώνει
μιὰ γκρίζα ἔχθρα

γιὰ ὅ,τι γειτονεύει μὲ τὴ φλόγα
κοίτα
ὣς καὶ τὴ μάνα της τὴ φωτιὰ
στάχτη τὴν ἔκανε

ὡστόσο στὴ στάχτη θὰ μ' ἐμπιστευτῶ

δὲν ἀφήνει λάσπης πατημασιὲς
στὸ σῶμα

ἀνάλαφρα σκορπίζεσαι
σὰ λίγη πούδρα ποὺ ἔχει μείνει
στὸ πρόσωπο τῆς βιογραφίας σου

στὴ στάχτη θὰ μ' ἐμπιστευτῶ

τὸ χῶμα μοῦ πέφτει βαρὺ

δὲν μπορεῖς ν' ἀνασάνεις
σὲ πιέζουν ἀπὸ πάνω καὶ οἱ γλάστρες
ποὺ φέρνουν οἱ δικοί σου

ESSENTIAL DIFFERENCE

Deep down I don't like ash

it is too intransigent
its manner conveys
a gray enmity

toward whatsoever lies close to a flame
look
it turned even fire, its own mother,
to ash

nonetheless to ash I will entrust myself

it leaves no muddy footprints
on the body

lightly you are scattered
like powder that has remained
on the face of your biography

to ash I will entrust myself

dirt is too great a burden

you can't breathe
compressed from above too by those flowerpots
your family brings—

βαραίνει καὶ τὸ πολὺ νερὸ ποὺ πίνουν

ἐσένα σὲ περονιάζει ἡ ὑγρασία
ἐχθρὸς γιὰ τὸ αὐχενικό σου

ἀλλὰ καὶ νὰ θέλεις νὰ πονέσεις
ἂν δὲν τὸ γράψεις κάπου
θὰ πάει διπλὰ χαμένο

ποῦ νὰ τὸ γράψεις

αὐτὸς ὁ μαυροπίνακας
δὲν εἶναι οὐρανὸς
κι ἐκεῖνο ποὺ ἀπέμεινε
δὲν εἶναι κιμωλία.

Στὴν τέφρα θὰ δοθῶ.

Βλέπεις τὸν κόσμο ἀλλιῶς
ὅταν ἀπὸ ψηλὰ σκορπίζεσαι

ἀναπνέεις πουλιὰ
μοσκοβολάει μυστήριο
βαθιὰ σὰν αἰθέρα σὲ μπαμπάκι
τὸ εἰσπνέεις
κι ἐκεῖνο σὰ μπαμπάκι σὲ ἀπορροφᾶ

σύννεφα θὰ σοῦ κρατοῦν

also heavy with all the water they drink in

you are chilled through by humidity
archenemy of your neck

but suppose you do want to feel the pain
if you don't write it down
it will be doubly wasted

where would you write it

this blackboard
is not sky
and what remains
is not chalk.

To ashes I will give myself.

You see the world differently
when scattered from above

you breathe birds
inhale the scent of mystery
of Sacrament deeply
like ether in cotton
and like cotton it absorbs you

clouds will carry

τὰ ἀναμνηστικά σου
βροχή, ὀμπρέλα, φάρμακα, τσιγάρα

φιλιὰ μὴν ξεχάσεις

ἀποκαΐδια γενικὰ

ἀσυζητητὶ μέσω τῆς στάχτης
ἐξάλλου

πάνω στ' ἀποκαΐδια σου
καὶ ξαναζήσει ἔχεις
καὶ ξαναγράψει ἔχεις
ἐπάνω τους τὰ ἴδια.

your mementos for you
rain, umbrella, medicine, cigarettes

let's not forget kisses

all these charred remains

in any case
indisputably through the ashes

on your charred remains
again you have lived
and again you have written
the very same things.

Η ΟΜΟΡΦΙΑ ΤΟΥ ΑΠΟΓΟΗΤΕΥΤΙΚΟΥ

Ὦ βλέμμα

λάθος κόσμο μοῦ γνώρισες.
Δὲν ἦταν αὐτός.

Ὦ ἀντίληψη

ἐὰν ὁ κόσμος ποὺ μοῦ γνώρισες ἐσὺ
εἶναι ὁ σωστὸς

δὲν ἦταν αὐτός.

Τὸ λάθος αἴσθημά μου
κι ὁ κόσμος του ὅλος

εἶν' ὁ σωστός μου κόσμος.

BEAUTY OF THE DISAPPOINTING

Oh gaze

you presented the wrong world to me.
It was not *the* one.

Oh perception

if the world you presented to me
is the right one

It was not *the* one.

My wrong feeling
and its whole world

is my right world.

ΜΟΝΟΗΜΕΡΗ ΜΕΡΑ

Ἂς κρυφτεῖ ὁ ἥλιος
πίσω ἀπ' τὸν καπνὸ ποὺ βγάζει
τὸ φουγάρο ἑνὸς ταξιδιοῦ
μὲ καράβι
ἢ μὲ ἐπιστολὴ
ἢ μὲ τὴν καύση τῆς ἐπιστολῆς

καὶ πίσω ἀπ' τὸν καπνὸ
ποὺ ἀνεβαίνει πουθενὰ
ἂς κρυφτεῖ ἡ ὥριμη αὐτὴ πράξη

ἂς κρυφτεῖ ὁ ἥλιος
καὶ πίσω ἀπὸ τὸ τεῖχος
τὸ ἀποδημητικὸ
ποὺ χτίζουν στὸν ἀέρα τὰ πουλιὰ

ἂς κρυφτεῖ
καὶ πίσω ἀπὸ ἕναν ἄνθρωπο
ποὺ δὲν ξυπνᾶ

μπορεῖ ποτὲ νὰ μὴ χορταίνεται ὁ ὕπνος

—ἕνας ὑπναρὰς νὰ εἶναι ὁ θάνατος

ἂς κρυφτεῖ ὁ ἥλιος

ἡ μέρα θέλει σήμερα

ONE-DAY DAY

May the sun hide
behind the smoke issuing
from the stack of a trip
by boat
or by letter
or by burning the letter

and behind the smoke
that climbs nowhere
may this ripe act hide

may the sun also hide
behind the wall
—a migratory wall—
birds build in the air

may it also hide
behind a man
who does not awaken

maybe we never get enough sleep

—maybe death is a sleepyhead

may the sun hide

today the day wants

λιτὰ νὰ ξοδευτεῖ

σὰν τρεμουλιαστὸ ἀνέβασμα

ἐλάχιστου καπνοῦ ἀπὸ μονοήμερο ταξίδι
πολὺ κοντινὸ
ὣς τὸ φάρο τοῦ γλάρου.

to be spent simply

like the quivering rising

of some tiny puffs of smoke from a day-trip
very close by
no farther than the seagull's lighthouse.

ΛΑΘΟΣ ΔΙΑΤΑΞΗ

Στὰ θαρραλέα φτερὰ μιᾶς σκέψης
ποὺ ἔχει σχέση ἀτρόμητη
καὶ μὲ τὰ πιὸ ἐπίφοβα
παντοδύναμα ὕψη

ἀνέθεσα
μιὰ καὶ μπαινοβγαίνει στὸ Θεὸ
μὲ τόση οἰκειότητα

νὰ τοῦ μεταφέρει
ὅτι αὐτὴ ἡ διάταξη

ἀπάνω ὁ οὐρανὸς
ὁλόκληρος νὰ τίθεται σκεπὴ
τῶν ἀοράτων

ἐνῶ ἡ γῆ κατάχαμα ἀφημένη
ὁλόκληρη ξεσκέπαστη νὰ εἶναι
ξέσκεπα ἀφήνοντας κι ὅλα τὰ ὁρατὰ

πῶς νὰ τὸ πῶ
δὲν εἶναι χριστιανικὴ

πρέπει
νὰ κατέβει κάτω ἐδῶ ὁ οὐρανὸς
ἡ γῆ νὰ καθρεφτίζεται σ' αὐτὸν
νὰ ὀμορφαίνει

•

WRONG ARRANGEMENT

To a brave-winged thought
which has an undaunted relationship
to even the most terrifying
of almighty heights

I gave the task
since it so casually goes
in and out of God's house

of conveying to him
that this arrangement

the whole sky above
set as a roof
over all things invisible

the earth flat on the ground
stripped bare
leaving bare all things visible

is, how shall I say,
unchristian

the sky
must come down here
so the earth will be mirrored there
and look more beautiful

•

κι ἐπειδὴ πεθαίνει
ἀκόμα κι ὁ καθρεφτισμὸς τῆς ὀμορφιᾶς

μέσα στὴ γῆ νὰ θάβεται
κι αὐτὸς

κι ἂν σπάζει κι ὁ καθρέφτης–οὐρανὸς
κατὰ τὴ μετακίνηση
κι ὅλα τὰ γύρω ὕψη
στὸ θρυψάλιασμά του παρασέρνει

ἐδῶ νὰ ἐνταφιάζονται
χάμω κι αὐτὰ τὰ θρύψαλα
δίπλα σὲ κάθε γήινο κλαδάκι τσακισμένο

ἔτσι πρέπει
δίπλα στὴν ἐπιδιόρθωσή της νὰ κεῖται
ἡ ἁρμονία τοῦ κόσμου

κι ἂν ὁ καθρέφτης εἶναι
σὲ κάθε παραλήρημα ἀπαραίτητος
κι ὄχι μονάχα στὸ δικό μου ἐτοῦτο

ἂς ἀνέβει ἡ γῆ
στὴ θέση τ᾽ οὐρανοῦ
σ᾽ αὐτὴν νὰ καθρεφτίζεται ὁ Θεὸς
γήινος, πιὸ καθημερινός, πιὸ ἀναγκαῖος.

and because even the mirroring
of beauty dies

it too should be buried
in the earth

and if the mirror-sky also breaks
splintering in transport
taking along with it
all the surrounding heights

here too should be interred
all these splinters
beside each small cracked earthly branch

and thus
world harmony should lie
by the side of its repair

and if the mirror is
necessary in each delirium
not only in this one of mine

let the earth climb
to the place of the sky
for God to be mirrored there
earthly, more commonplace, more indispensable.

ΥΠΕΡΒΑΣΗ

Πόσο ἔχω ἐπιθυμήσει
δεμένη στὸ ἕνα ἔστω φτερὸ
κάποιου μεγάλου ταξιδιάρικου πουλιοῦ

ξαπλωτὴ ὄχι ἀνάσκελα
γιατὶ τὰ ὑπεράνω μου
ὅλα σχεδὸν τὰ ἔχω δεῖ

μπρούμυτα δεμένη στὸ ἕνα φτερὸ

νὰ φωτογραφίσω
ἂν εἶναι ἀπὸ τὸ ἴδιο ὑλικὸ φτιαγμένες
οἱ σκεπές μας

καὶ σὺ μὲ ταπεινώνεις, μοῦ λὲς

ὅτι κανένα πουλὶ
μὲ ἀχρηστευμένο τὸ ἕνα φτερό του
ἀπὸ τὸ βάρος μου
δὲ διακινδυνεύει τέτοιο ταξίδι

λάθος κάνεις

ἔχω πολλὲς φορὲς ψηλὰ πετάξει
στὸ βάρος μου δεμένη.

TRANSCENDENCE

How I wish —
bound at least to one wing
of some large bird of passage

not lying on my back
since I have seen
almost all things above me

rather on my stomach bound to one wing —

to take photographs and check whether
our roofs
are made of the same material

but you humiliate me, you say

that no bird
with one wing impaired
by my weight
would risk such a trip

you are mistaken

many times I have flown high
bound to my own weight.

ΣΑΤΑΝΙΚΗ ΣΥΜΠΤΩΣΗ

Ἡ ἀνυπομονησία
ἡ καμιὰ ἀπολύτως βιασύνη
ὁ τρόπος τοῦ λέγειν
ὁ τρόπος τοῦ σιωπᾶν
ἡ ἐπιμονὴ
ἡ εὔσχημη ὑποχωρητικότητα
τὸ ζωηρὸ ἐνδιαφέρον
τὸ ράθυμο ἐνδιαφέρον
τὸ ἀμέσως
τὸ κόμπιασμα
τὸ ἐξαρτᾶται ἀπ' τὸν καιρὸ
τὸ ἀσχέτως καιροῦ
τὸ πολὺ ἐπιθυμητὸ
τὸ ἀξεκαθάριστα ἐπιθυμητὸ
καὶ τὸ κατ' ἀνάγκην

ἔχουν τὸν ἴδιο ἀκριβῶς κωδικό:

ἀλήθεια πότε θὰ σὲ δῶ;

DIABOLICAL COINCIDENCE

The impatience
the no haste at all
the so to speak
the not speaking
the insistence
the spurious compliance
the vivid interest
the sluggish interest
the instantly
the hemming and hawing
the depending on the weather
the in all kinds of weather
the very desirable
the indefinably desirable
and the by necessity

all share the exact same code:

tell me, when will I see you?

ΤΟ ΡΕΜΑΛΙ

Καταζητοῦμαι.
Διέρρηξα τὸ βίο μου.
Τί νὰ ἔκανα;
Μόνο μὲ τὰ ξένα δὲν τὰ ἔβγαζα πέρα
εἶχα βλέπεις νὰ τρέφω
ἐκεῖνο τὸ ρεμάλι τὸν ψυχισμό.

Καὶ τί βρῆκα
ἕνα δυὸ πρωινά, ἀπὸ λίγο τὸ καθένα
σὲ φλιτζανάκι τοῦ καφὲ νὰ φανταστεῖς
δυὸ τρία ἀπογεύματα μέσα
στὸ βιαστικὸ φέρετρό τους
καὶ σὲ ταπεράκι
ἀδιάβαστη, χωρὶς ψαλμὸ χωρὶς θεὸ
ἡ τέφρα μιᾶς ματαιωμένης ἐκδρομῆς
σὲ κεῖνο τὸ μαγευτικὸ ἐρημονήσι
μιᾶς κοντινῆς ὑπόσχεσής σου.

Αὐτὰ καὶ ποιὸ τὸ κέρδος;
Μόλις τὰ εἶδε ὁ κλεπταποδόχος
εἶπε
συνηθισμένα πράγματα
ἐγὼ δὲν ἀγοράζω.

THE GOOD-FOR-NOTHING

I'm wanted by the police
I broke into my own life.
What else could I do?
I couldn't manage just by borrowing
you see, I had my good-for-nothing
psyche to feed.

And what did I find
one or two mornings, a bit of each
in a small coffee cup, imagine,
two or three afternoons in
their rushing coffin
and in a little Tupperware,
without funeral, hymn, or god
the ashes of a canceled trip
to the enchanting desert island
of a nearby promise you gave me.

What profit from these?
When the fence saw them
he said
"common junk
no sale."

ΜΠΡΟΣΤΑ Σ' ΕΝΑ ΕΠΙΤΡΑΠΕΖΙΟ ΗΜΕΡΟΛΟΓΙΟ

ΜΕΣΑΝΥΧΤΑ

Πέθανες ἀπὸ ἕνα σήμερα ἀκαριαῖο
ἀγαπημένη μου ἡμέρα.

Κόσμιο θάνατο ἐπέδειξες
δὲν καταδέχτηκες νὰ τὸν καθυστερήσεις

μὲ καλοπιάσματα
ἀφιερώνοντάς του ποιήματα

οὔτε μὲ παρακάλια πὼς ἔχεις μιὰ ἀνήλικη
ἀγάπη ν' ἀναθρέψεις καὶ ποῦ θὰ τὴν ἀφήσεις.

Σὲ κοιτάζω τώρα ξαπλωμένη
σὲ ὕπτια στάση, ἀνάσκελα
πάνω στὸ ἄγραφο ἀτσαλάκωτο
φύλλο τοῦ ἡμερολογίου

στὸ μαξιλάρι ἀκουμπᾶς τὸ κεντημένο
μὲ τὸ μονόγραμμά σου: δεκαοχτὼ
Ἰανουάριος δύο χιλιάδες δέκα

πόσο γαλήνια δείχνεις, νεανικὴ

ἄσβηστο ἀκόμα ὣς καὶ τὸ ροδαλὸ
ἐκεῖνο ξάναμμα στὴν ὄψη
ποὺ σοῦ προκαλοῦσε ἡ μεγάλη ἀνηφοριὰ

IN FRONT OF A DESK DIARY
MIDNIGHT

You died of an instantaneous today
my dearest day.

You displayed dignity
not condescending to delay your death

with coaxing
dedicatory poems

nor by pleading that you have an underage
love to bring up and where to leave it.

Day, I look at you now
lying flat on your back
on the smooth blank
diary page

you rest on the pillow embroidered
with your monogram: eighteen
January two thousand ten

how peaceful you seem, young

still glowing, even the pink
flush on your cheeks
brought on by the steep ascent

πρὸς τὴν ἀνατολή σου.

Ἀπὸ τὰ τρομερὰ ποὺ ἔζησες διασχίζοντας
αἰῶνες ὥσπου στὸ σήμερα νὰ φτάσεις
τίποτα δὲ φαίνεται

σὰν ἀγάπη ἀνήλικη ἀπείραχτη φαντάζεις.

Ἂς εἶναι ἐλαφρὺ τὸ φύλλο
τῆς αὐριανῆς ἡμέρας ποὺ τὸ γυρίζω τώρα
νὰ σὲ σκεπάσει
μπρούμυτα πιὰ πεσμένη.

toward your dawn.

Of the horrors endured, passing
through centuries to reach today
nothing shows

you resemble an innocent, underage love.

May tomorrow's page
that I'm turning now
be light and cover you
while you lie face down.

CHRONOLOGY

Cecile Inglessis Margellos

"A biographical note, once it's been written, should be left hanging in the air from severity's hook for quite some time, where it can be drained of stereotypes, embellishments, rosy productivity, and added narcissism — on top of that inherent in the very nature of self-presentation. Only then do you get the net weight: the moral standard your effort was driven to keep." — Kiki Dimoula

1931
June 6: Vassiliki Radou (later Kiki Dimoula) is born in Athens at 42 Pythia Street to Eleni Kalamarioti and Christos Rados, a Bank of Greece employee. She later described her mother, a housewife, as "extremely melancholy": "Because of a peculiar situation in our family, she never went out. We lived with her two bachelor brothers, remarkable but neurotic creatures, who reduced her to a spectacular slavery. One of them [Panayotis Kalamariotis], a lawyer, could not stay home alone, so she shut herself in with him." As for her father: "[He] was a quiet man who didn't meddle in our future, only in the morality of the present. In that respect he was a terrorist."

1940
Sister Dimitra is born.

1945
Meets Athos (Athanasios) Dimoulas (b. 1921), a young civil engineer and poet, the son of her high school Greek teacher. He lives down the road from her, at 26 Pythia Street. Athos tutors Kiki and her classmates in math. "My school record was mediocre; I was only good at composition, at math my grades were below zero! I didn't study. I liked to sing, and at night I fantasized about being on a stage with the audience tossing flowers at me."

1949

A few months after graduation from high school, following the example of her father and two of her uncles, she goes to work as a clerk for the Bank of Greece, where she will remain until her retirement twenty-five years later. "Every morning the same thing. From 8 A.M. to 3 P.M. And these were times most unfavorable to women. The blue pinafore with the white collar we had to wear was the least of our troubles. The worst was that our bosses terrorized us. They would spy on us from every corner to make sure we were working."

1950

June 15: The prestigious literary magazine *Nea Hestia* (New Hearth) publishes two of her poems under the name Kiki Chr. Radou.

1952

As a gift for her name day (January 1) her uncle Panayotis Kalamariotis, a constant source of coaching and encouragement, privately publishes a volume of her poetry, titled *Poems*. (She will soon silently disavow this book, which will not be included in her 1998 collection, *Poems*.) "It was this uncle who probably taught me how to use the Greek language. It was he who took the scribblings I kept in a drawer—I must have been about seventeen— and printed them." The young poet, who still goes by the name Kiki Chr. Radou, is welcomed by the influential writer and critic Petros Haris with a laudatory review: "We have the first and major sign of a truly new voice."

1954

May: Marries Athos Dimoulas, whose three collections of poems have already attracted attention. "He was my step, my feet, my hands, my wholeness. As a young girl I was shaped at his side. Had I married some other man with no notion about poetry, I might not even have continued. But he wanted me to be a poet. So I had to meet his expectations." The couple live in Athos's family home, sharing it with Athos's mother until her death. "I was living in a house I didn't want to live in, making unsuccessful attempts to move out. Let me give you an example of how one can stray from one's destiny: After thirty years spent on Pythia Street with Athos Dimoulas, I managed to convince both myself and him to move. So I bought an apartment in Agia Paraskevi [a northeastern suburb of Athens]. He didn't want to go—I did, like crazy. I fixed it up, we carried cartons of books there, we moved, and six months later we left and moved back to Pythia Street, from which I had always wanted to escape."

1955
Son Dimitris is born. (Today he is a mathematician working for the Bank of Greece, a literary translator, and the father of two.)

1956
Publishes *Erebus*, which she considers her first true collection of poems. Both title and content owe much to the dark, if trenchantly ironic, pessimism of the poet Kostas Karyotakis, an emblematic figure of 1920s Greece who committed suicide in 1928. Yet several features of Dimoula's poetics are already present, notably the animation of the inanimate ("I imagine Dionysos / carefully rising from his stand"), the personification of material entities ("the window takes me into its embrace"), and, conversely, the reification of immaterial ones ("a handful of cloudmist"). The writer Takis Doxas remarks that she is "fully aware of what is superfluous and of the verse's sobriety. She philosophizes aphoristically, feels aphoristically, enunciates aphoristically."

1957
Daughter Elsi is born. (Today she is a philologist working for the Bank of Greece, the mother of two, and her mother's ubiquitous chaperon and most exacting editor.)

1958
In Absentia is published. In this new collection, a deeply rooted self-irony emerges. In "Utopias," for instance, the speaker identifies herself with spring, but the elation is brief:

> I plant myself with flowers,
> blossom with feelings,
> and feel very well
> within my boundless destination
> and position.
>
> "Spring Prohibited!"
> suddenly a sign — a cloud —
> threatens.

Dimoula's ingenious amalgamation of the literal and the metaphorical already marks its presence when she goes on to describe herself as "a woman of a certain age, / who has . . . many years of service / to the public / and to winter." Anthropomorphic abstractions gradually invade her poetic realm, as in the self-referential "Transfer," in which the speaker's works—the offspring of the dead "today"—are described as "orphans and minors" being prepared for their "stepmother": "the day to come."

1959

Ho Kyklos (The Circle), a literary magazine written by employees of the Bank of Greece, is founded by the writer and translator Nasos Detzortzis, another Bank employee. Dimoula is on the editorial committee and publishes op-ed pieces and short stories in the magazine (collected in 2004 as *Unplanned*).

1960

Two of her poems are published in *Kainourgia Epochi* (New Era) magazine. Dimoula impresses—sometimes shocks—her readers with her atypical and bold interweaving of the vernacular (demotic) and the formal archaic Greek (*katharevousa*), which was then the official language. The poet Melpo Axioti writes to her colleague Yannis Ritsos, perhaps Greece's most famous poet at the time: "In *Kainourgia Epochi* there are two excellent poems by the unknown to me Kiki Dimoula, which I almost didn't read because her name is Kiki [a somewhat plebeian diminutive of Vassiliki]. Rarely in our days has the katharevousa managed to bring to the fore so effectively the dramatic element of a satire." Linguistically eclectic and politically neutral, Dimoula eschews George Seferis' poetic and political stance in favor of an unalloyed demotic, at the time a symbol of the Greek cultural renaissance.

1963

Publication of her new collection of poems, *On the Track*. Critics talk of a camouflaged romanticism "that wears the mask of anti-romantic prosiness." With its parodic linguistic preciosity and its intermingling of personal anecdote and detached meditativeness, the book is somewhat Cavafyan in scope and tone. But Dimoula's artistry in deploying the manifold significations of trivial images is unprecedented. As in her stunning "Easter, Toward Sounion":

And right there, a gloomy shrine
encloses a Christ, apparently unrisen.
For on him a plastic wreath
still forgotten
prolongs the passion of the Cross.

A naive devotional scene revealing a dual paradox: endlessly prolonged, this crucifixion leads to no resurrection, no new life, while spring—nature's annual rebirth—is symbolized by lifeless synthetic flowers. But there is also a mordant irony in the fact that Christ's Passion seems to culminate in the unredeemable kitsch of a plastic wreath. As the writer Tasos Hatzitatsis described it, "Dimoula's daring and luminous verse manages to transcend the influence of poetic tradition (Cavafy, Rilke, Athos Dimoulas, surrealists—all of them men) and give us an authentic, native art, with feminine endings and articles. A demon poetry, a double-edged knife raised menacingly above our ancestral, male sins, but articulated harmoniously in the katharevousa of our imagination."

1967
The Greek Junta, which has recently taken over the government, closes down *Ho Kyklos* because it is considered Marxist.

1971
The Little of the World, which announces her mature style and unquestionably establishes her as a major poet, is published. "Whatever I wrote [up until then] was written on the trolley bus, on my way back and forth from the bank where I used to work. The first book I wrote sitting at a desk was *The Little of the World*. It was around for quite a few years and nothing happened, until all of a sudden people started talking about it." The motif of the photograph and its relation to time, memory, and loss, which had made a discreet first appearance in the previous collection, is omnipresent in this new book, for instance in "Photograph 1948":

I'm probably holding a flower.
Strange.
A garden must have gone
through my life once.

1972
The Little of the World wins her Greece's Second National Poetry Prize. As she later explains: "I live *in* my century, but I live my century very little. And I found a way—who knows if it's mine?—to speak for every 'Little.'" The book is indeed a sotto voce celebration of every "little," for instance, the word *or*. The beautiful poem "The Disjunctive *Or*" is a meditation on the existential intimations of this tiny conjunction:

> rain or tears,
> love or a way of growing old,
> you or the little dangling farewell
> of the last leaf's shadow.

1974
February: Retires from the Bank of Greece. "I felt that my job had become something definitive, and this weighed upon me. Because one always thinks one is meant for something else. Although one knows not what. Yet, I don't think this millstone kept my poetry from going farther than it was destined to go or that it imprisoned its themes."

March 12: Her father dies.

1981
My Last Body is published. A growing disillusionment, perhaps due to the first marks of aging and to her husband's illness (Athos has been diagnosed with prostate cancer), transforms Dimoula's poems into poignant allegories of vanity—the scriptural equivalent of a Georges de La Tour *Vanitas*. But the counterpart of this existential angst is an often acerbic demystifying strategy. The poet Sotiris Tsampiras notes that Dimoula sidesteps the danger of melodrama by "easily inserting into her verses prosaic words and phrases—quotidian and often slangy—that have a comical or satirical overtone." Consider the rakish invective uttered by the solemn abstraction Experience: "You must be kidding, great Experience / chuckled."

1985
September 28: Athos Dimoulas dies, after five years of suffering and numerous trips to London for treatment. Dimoula mourns, "His death cut off my arms and legs, rendered me useless, made me too scared to go out,

to meet people. I never got over this interruption of our coexistence." Nine years later: "This grief will not subside. Precisely because the loss is so great, it manages, little by little, to resemble existence. And I don't mean those ghosts born out of memories. No. It's something like a methodical effort, on the part of the deceased, to live on. For his own sake."

1986

April 26: Death of her mother. "My mother's passing left me feeling very much the orphan in my fifties. I have no one to turn to anymore, no one with patience. A mother is the only one patient enough to listen to you, to keep listening to you for all time. No one else." Asked to provide additional information about her mother and father for the present volume, Dimoula humorously noted: "My parents would have never dreamt that someday their totally Greek death would be translated into English."

1988

Publication of a new volume of poetry, *Hail Never*, in memory of Athos. "His death gave me something to write about, even though it pains me to invoke it." Reviewing this collection, the poet Tasos Roussos notes, "The poet, one of the most important voices in Greece today, works with the most difficult, the most uninspiring material: with the grammatical, the unmythologized meanings of words. She opens these deadened shells and reveals the sparkling pearl hidden in their depths. Indeed, I will dare call this a sort of *surrealism of grammar and syntax.* These abstract concepts that pose such a mortal danger to poetry are transformed into sensitive beings throbbing with life and taking us on magical flights." Thus, "an empty room is blowing," "vertigo smells sweet," afternoons become "alcoholic," and "words grow green." Dimoula's vitalism fascinates literary critics as well as an ever growing number of faithful readers.

1989

Awarded Greece's highest literary prize for a single book of poems, the First National Poetry Prize, for *Hail Never*.

1990

December: In a widely cited article, the writer Nikos Dimou postulates that Dimoula "talks about darkness, nonbeing, nothingness, things that cannot be said—and yet she says them. While most poets are crushed when trying to tackle the abstract, Dimoula is able to create philosophical poetry as tangible as a clump of earth and as metaphysical as apophatic theology." Dimou astutely compares Dimoula to the seventeenth-century English metaphysicals, but he also associates her with Emily Dickinson, her "spiritual sister": "Strange—when nothingness wants to talk, it now chooses women. Perhaps because they are braver than men."

1994
Oblivion's Adolescence is published, "dedicated to Athos again." Dimoula's work is now attracting the attention of younger and more skeptical postmodernist literati, such as the poet Evgenios Aranitsis, who notes: "What is there left to be written using the glittering metaphors of a prosaic life? A longing for an intimacy with the reader and for confession can be faintly seen here. The poem is still an 'oracle,' but its emotive radiance, more distinctive than ever, illuminates the scene of a reality more 'prosaic,' more familiar, more 'hackneyed': enchantment no longer chases after the stars, but has in a way installed itself in the city, in the streets, in the houses, in the embrace of things . . . ; what we have here, then, is a spectral sadness that brushes against the parody of all the beautiful things we have loved, against the living cell of a wise and desperate sense of humor." Thus the collection's emblematic title poem subtly ridicules and at the same time regrets the idealization that distance—whether literal or figurative, physical or rhetorical—affords:

> What would the stars be
> without the help of Distance?
> Earthly flatware, candlestick ashtrays.
> ["Oblivion's Adolescence"]

1995
Receives the Ouranis Prize of the Academy of Athens for *Oblivion's Adolescence*. In a speech at Arsakeion high school, Dimoula describes her sense of her own poetry: "I don't feel I'm an artist. I believe I'm a trustworthy stenographer of a very rushed anxiety, which at times calls to me and, hidden in the dim light of a delirium, whisperingly, incoherently, spasmodically dictates its debaucheries with an unknown way of life. Only when I begin to rewrite am I forced to intervene: wherever words, whole phrases, and

often the meaning of this orgy are missing, I add my own words, my own phrases, my own orgy to the meaning—in short, whatever's left over of my own debaucheries with another, unknown way of life."

1996

The first volume exclusively devoted to Dimoula's poetry in English translation, *Lethe's Adolescence*—an anthology of poems from her two most recent volumes—is published. In his introduction, the translator, David Connolly, notes, "The poems in these two collections represent a painful opening and examination of the wound left by loss, with the resulting catharsis. They attempt to convey grief in an original way, devoid of sentimentalism and lyrical threnody. They are far from the kind of poems Seferis referred to as 'emotional evaporations.' Her avoidance of sentimentality no doubt testifies to the influence of her husband, who consciously attempted to keep his own poetry free of all sentimental or mellifluous elements."

1998

October: Leaves her publisher Stigmi for the prestigious Ikaros (home to the Nobel laureates George Seferis and Odysseas Elytis), which produces a volume of her collected poems (excluding the disavowed 1952 collection) under the title *Poems*, as well as a new volume of poems, *A Moment of Two*, once more dedicated to Athos Dimoulas. The peculiar and grammatically irregular Greek title, *Enos leptou mazi* (literally: "one minute's together") is a play on the common expression *enos leptou sigi* ("one minute's silence"). "First of all it's a mistake," Dimoula explained, "a distortion of 'a minute's silence.' 'A minute's silence' means that we observe a minute of silence in someone's memory, that we remember someone for one minute. 'A minute's together' means the same thing: that whatever happens in the world happens so that we can be together for one minute; that neither euphoria nor happiness lasts for more than a minute." The English title, *A Moment of Two*, playing—by virtue of a single letter change—on "a moment or two," re-creates, if imperfectly, this wordplay, paradox (a moment composed of two moments), and equivocity (two moments or two people). It is meant to underscore the implacable brevity of a couple's togetherness—the cardinal intimation of Dimoula's title. Discussing emblematic poems from Dimoula's volume such as "Incident," "Reversal of the Reasonable," and "Saint Lazarus' Day," the poet Nikos Davvetas writes, "The common traits:

a slightly metaphysical climate; essential questions (usually addressed to the Creator) that enhance the sense of tragedy since, of course, they remain unanswered; symbols and imagery from the large pool of Christian myths."

By now a major public figure, Dimoula represents a real paradox, for despite the complexity of her poetry, she enjoys the celebrity of a pop singer. This is in part because, as happens only with great literary works, her poems are addressed to a wide range of readers and lend themselves to various levels of reading. As a result her book sales reach figures never before achieved by collections of poetry, and the interest in her life and deeds is evidenced by an increasing demand for interviews in major newspapers and magazines. Describing the phenomenon she calls "the whip of popularity" Dimoula has said: "Popularity is somewhat incompatible with being a poet, isn't it? A very good singer is popular. A very good comedian is popular. We never referred to Elytis as a popular poet, even though he had a very wide public and enjoyed huge recognition. But he escaped the smear of popularity. As moving as it is to be popular, I can't help but wonder what's going on with the people who love me or delude themselves that they love me."

2001

March 22: Presented with the Aristeion of Letters of the Academy of Athens in recognition of her complete oeuvre. The award, given for the first time to a woman, is seen by the press as paving the way for her induction into the Academy of Athens.

May: Publication of *Sound of Distancings*. "Distancing myself from something means approaching something else. Melancholy as the title may sound, there is movement inherent in it. I don't believe a seat empties and remains vacant. I distance myself from, say, a hope, means I approach the certainty that we can live without it." The poems have become heartrending appeals, often in the form of an apostrophe to or a dramatic dialogue with the dead, the inanimate, or the absent—the deceased companion or mother, rain, or a friend living abroad. Constitutionally absent (and, of course, all personae of the constitutionally absent reader), disembodied, or bodiless, these figures are more substantial and incarnate than if they were present. The distance that separates them from the real, the living, the *hic et nunc*, is easy to cover in the blink of an eye or, better still, in the blink of a verse:

Yes, please put my mother on.
What number did I call? The sky's —
that's the one they gave me. Not there?
Can I scream a message to her?
["I Left You a Message"]

The poet's quotidian, conversational mode eliminates this distance, as does the often sarcastic and self-deprecating tone, mitigating the morbidity of a quasi-spiritualistic communication.

2002

February 23: Elected a full member of the Academy of Athens, Order of Letters. "I still haven't overcome my terror of how unequipped I always am, arriving at the threshold of this most high, intense, solid, and by no means indiscriminately trumpeted intellectuality throbbing inside there. I don't feel at all like the fairytale emperor who, while walking around naked, deludes himself into thinking he's wearing splendid clothes." To the journalist Olga Bakomarou, when asked how it felt to be an "immortal" academician: "The word makes me feel melancholy, because there is also something darkly humorous about it. What's this 'immortal'? It's more an accent on 'mortal' than some other reality. . . . The idea that we are mortal rather than immortal is a mortal blow to me. At the same time, I am left speechless at how miraculously we appear to forget this fate of ours."

November 11: At the ceremony for her induction into the Academy of Athens, she delivers a speech, published in December as *The Frolicsome Fable*, in which she draws a cunningly modest self-portrait: "I'm not a thinking person. Just a little thoughtful, which also means absent-mindedly surprised and fatalistically incomplete. I'm more a physical mind, an observant body, which simply possesses organs by which to precisely measure the instantaneous, and an automatic, old-fashioned needless to say, diagnostic instinct."

2004

November: Publication of *Unplanned*, the selection of (sparkling, witty precociously profound) op-ed pieces and short stories first published in the Bank of Greece's *Ho Kyklos* magazine (1959–67).

2005

April: Publication of *Greenhouse Grass*, whose title Dimoula explains thus: "I desire. A patch of grass. And if it's greenhouse grass, all the better. Which is to say, a duel with the impossible. . . . The fact that I desire doesn't mean that I have disavowed vanity and the ephemeral. But neither one is such a devil that it can tempt us to deny our love of life and the desires this love engenders."

2006

Moves almost literally next door, from 26 Pythia Street to 26 Phaethon Street, to an apartment vacated by her daughter Elsi, who had lived there since 1998. Despite the short distance, the move is a painful one, which inspires the title of her next collection, *We've Moved Next Door.* An entire life has been lived and will continue to be lived on two streets and in three houses, which together inscribe a square. Or a circle. A unique geographical (and numerical) immutability. A stasis containing its own mystical dynamic, which propels not horizontally but vertically, upwardly, and is imbued by a special symbolism. Dimoula has never strayed from her Delphi. (Let us not forget that Phaethon was the son of Apollo.) A modern-day high priestess of the Sun God, or of the pre-Apollonian Delphic deity Gaia, Dimoula has turned her neighborhood into the omphalos—the very navel—of the earth. There she is free to prophesize, thanks to the vapors of familiar things and faces, the fumes of mind-altering memories (and four dozen cigarettes a day).

2007

March: Ikaros publishes *Encounter: Jannis Psychopedis—Kiki Dimoula.* The painter Psychopedis chose eighty of Dimoula's poems, selected from *Erebus* to *Greenhouse Grass*, and illustrated them with seventy-three original paintings, explaining, "In terms of painting, Kiki Dimoula's poetry is like an existential kind of pop art, with a powerful reference to a reality completely overthrown, so as to lead to transcendence."

November: *We've Moved Next Door* is published. "Its title . . . especially alludes to the generally immovable nature of some people's psychological makeup. The occasion was an actual move I made to another house, with modern facilities and comforts, a lift, a view, a door phone and, more important, not a stranger's house, but a house warmed up by the fact that my children had lived there. They have lived happily ever after, and so have I. Together with them." Critics have seldom noticed that this book is also—or perhaps mainly—love poetry, if poignantly disenchanted:

> Every kiss
> consists entirely of the risk
> it may be the last.
>
> Only the kiss never given
> remains everlasting.
> ["Epitaph"]

As she later describes her attitude toward love, or, rather, the more precise and at the same time more inclusive life impulse that Greeks since Hesiodic times have called eros: "Why do you call me a pessimist? On the contrary, when you asked me for the umpteenth time what Eros is, I concealed Lamentations' opinion about this ever rekindled feeling."

2009
January 16: Gives a speech to the Athens Archaeological Society, published by Ikaros later that year as *Thoughtraising for the Erection of a Title to House This Homeless Speech:* "I tally countless blotting-paper shipwrecks, loaded with tons of absorbent writing. So when they ask me 'What is poetry?' I answer with melancholy honesty: 'If I knew, would I have been shipwrecked?'"

November: Awarded the European Prize for Literature by the Association Capitale Européenne des Littératures (ACEL).

2010
March: Michel Volkovitch's translation of *The Little of the World* and *Hail Never* is published by the venerable Éditions Gallimard, making Dimoula the first living female poet in the Poésie Gallimard series. (The same year, Gallimard also publishes an anthology of the fifteen female poets in the series, which significantly and symbolically starts with Sappho and ends with Dimoula, thereby confirming the perennial lineage of great Greek female lyrical poets.)

By now, Dimoula's poetry has been translated into numerous languages: Albanian, Bulgarian, Danish, English, Finnish, French, German, Italian, Polish, Serbian, Spanish, Swedish—both in individual poetry collections and in various anthologies. Her poems have been set to music by the major contemporary Greek composer Thanos Mikroutsikos (1998), and by Nikos Xanthoulis (2002), Kyriakos Sfetsas (2002), and Christos Dalkos (2002), among others.

At the presentation ceremony for the European Prize for Literature in Strasbourg, where Michel Volkovitch wins the E.P.L.'s 2010 translation grant, Dimoula gives one of her most eloquent and moving definitions of poetry: "You walk in a desert. You hear a bird singing. Incredible as it may be that a bird should be hovering over the desert, you have to make a tree for it. That's what a poem is."

May: Publication of *The Finder's Reward:* "These poems were written as if I returned to an old sentiment, which I had found sometime in the past, completely uninhabited, I had moved into it, then I was kicked out, and now I've come back and, finding it empty once more, consistently uninhabited, I've refurbished it with what I wrote." At the peak of her creativity, Dimoula becomes "physically" metaphysical. She requests that the old Platonic and Christian hierarchy, by which celestial perfection is mirrored in the earth (what the philosopher Gaston Bachelard calls cosmic narcissism), be reversed:

> the sky
> must come down here
> so the earth will be mirrored there
> and look more beautiful.

She upends and at the same time takes to extremes the humanistic reading of God's word in Genesis, "Let us make man in our image, after our likeness," by putting the earth in the place of the sky and by anthropomorphizing God instead of "theomorphizing" man:

> let the earth climb
> to the place of the sky
> for God to be mirrored there
> earthly, more commonplace, more indispensable.
> ["Wrong Arrangement"]

Even the relationship between writing and duration is subject to a similar upending. Writing is not the guarantor of our perpetuation, the recorder of our memory and actions—that *ktema es aei* (possession of all time) that Thucydides spoke of. On the contrary, it is the copyist of the ephemeral, counterfeiting a deceptive durability. Writing is

> A brazen unholy plagiarist
>
> it copies
> both speaking and ceasing to exist
> expertly forged as
> lasting.
> ["The Brazen Plagiarist"]

The paradox is that writing is said to be unholy not because it denies immortality but because it sustains an illusion of immortality through a dubious eternity made of paper. But is that so paradoxical? Dimoula's anti-logic hides an implacable constitutive logic: all that is written, at the precise moment it is written, is already past, dead. The transmutation through writing—through poetry—of the dead into the living presupposes the dead. In that sense, poetry is a "study" or, better, a "practice of death," as is philosophy, according to Socrates in Plato's *Phaedo*. After all, before drinking the hemlock the philosopher also wrote poetry, obeying the dream which urged him to "make and cultivate music."

In *The Finder's Reward*, despite or perhaps because of her Beckettian pessimism, Dimoula's humor is ever more corrosive. As in the bloodcurdling albeit hilariously funny "Essential Difference":

> to ash I will entrust myself
>
> dirt is too great a burden
>
> you can't breathe
> compressed from above too by those flowerpots
> your family brings—
> also heavy with all the water they drink in
>
> you are chilled through by humidity
> archenemy of your neck.

2011

Receives the Grand National Prize for lifetime achievement, Greece's most distinguished literary award. On whether her award means anything to Greek society, she comments, "How society perceives matters of art in general depends on how far its soul has accepted the belief that art, poetry in this case, will not impose cutbacks on the escape it provides. That it gives a loan, and indeed an interest-free loan, to every case of bankrupt courage. I really don't know what percentage of society needs this vital loan. But I meet plenty of people who are moved by poetry and grateful to it for changing their life. And I have no trouble disappointing them by telling them that, oddly enough, my life doesn't change at all, other than during the hours I spend walking my feet off outside poetry, waiting for it to come out."

June 6: When asked by the columnist Dimitris Politakis on her eightieth birthday whether she has "rightfully earned a certain maturity," Dimoula replies, "No, not rightfully. I didn't earn maturity; it was imposed on me by time. A maturity which, of course, has nothing to do with that of fruit. A fruit is eaten when it's mature—which is to say when it's ripe. Whereas my maturity cannot be eaten, but eats away at me instead."

2012

March 17: Dimoula, who has kept away from politics though the social and existential dimension of the political deeply concerns and affects her, comments on the Greek crisis: "This messiness and irresponsibility of all things drives me crazy. What drives me crazy most of all is a category to which I don't belong (my reaction is far from humanitarian): people who are homeless and people who are receiving 300-euro pensions. That makes me feel ashamed. I cannot get used to the fact that there are people sleeping in the street. As if being reduced to homelessness by our fate alone were not quite enough, we must also experience in advance this enactment of what it means to be homeless—it's just unbearable."

And yet, "I believe that long-term crises give much power to hope. We don't need to know what we're hoping for. It is this very ambiguity that helps us endure. If we were told that we would agonize for five days, the utter specificity would make even this short time intolerable. Patience draws courage from not knowing how many kilometers of trials and tribulations lie before it."

My warm thanks to Yorgos Kordomenidis for allowing me to make wide use of his meticulous chronology published in *Enteuktirio* 83 (October–December 2008), whose entire issue was dedicated to the work of Kiki Dimoula. The quotations from Kiki Dimoula are excerpted from various interviews and speeches, as well as thoughts she generously shared with me over the years.

NOTES

Easter, Toward Sounion

Cape Sounion: a spectacular promontory forty-three miles SSE of Athens, site of an ancient temple of Poseidon. According to the legend, Aegeus, king of Athens, jumped off the cliff of Cape Sounion when he saw the black sail—a sign that his son Theseus had been killed fighting the Minotaur—on the ship that brought the victorious hero back from Crete.

Allusions are made to the Feast of Pentecost and to Mark 16:1, 4.

The Little of the World

Reference is made to John 1:29, "Behold, the Lamb of God, which taketh away the sin of the world!"

Chronicle of the Fruit and the Unfruitful

Mystras: a medieval fortified city situated in the southeastern Peloponnese, in the vicinity of Sparta (Lacedaemon), and the capital of the Byzantine Despotate of the Morea (medieval name for the Peloponnese). In the fourteenth and fifteenth centuries, it enjoyed great economic and cultural prosperity. In 1989 it was named a UNESCO World Heritage Site.

Peribleptos: a fourteenth-century monastery in Mystras, now in ruins, dedicated to the Virgin Mary Peribleptos (visible from all over, prominent). It is famous for its magnificent late-Byzantine frescoes.

Polychronion: a Greek Orthodox ecclesiastical hymn, wishing "many years" or "long life" to eminent secular or church dignitaries.

Palaiologos: a member of the Byzantine Greek noble family of the Palaiologoi, the last ruling dynasty of the Byzantine Empire. Constantine XI Palaiologos (1404–1453) was despot of the Morea before he was crowned (last) emperor of the Byzantine Empire at Mystras in 1449. He was killed in battle during the fall of Constantinople to the Ottoman Turks in 1453. According to Greek legend, however, he did not die but was turned into marble, waiting to awaken to recapture Constantinople and the empire.

Sweetest Uncertainty

The poem opens with the word Τρισάγια, plural of Τρισάγιον (*Trisagion:* Thrice Holy). The Trisagion Service is an abbreviated memorial service, including psalms and prayers of the Funeral Service. It gets its name from the triple invocation Ἅγιος, Ἅγιος, Ἅγιος (*Hagios:* Holy). Dimoula refers to the following lines: "Oh Lord, give rest to the soul of Thy servant who has fallen asleep in a place of brightness, a place of refreshment, a place of repose, from which all sickness, sorrow and sighing have fled away."

Hail Never

Salutations: Χαιρετισμοί (*Chairetismoi:* Salutations) are part of the Greek Orthodox *Akathist Hymn* to the Holy Virgin, a long hymn of praise and thanksgiving, chanted on the first five consecutive Fridays of Lent. They are introduced by the word Χαῖρε (*Chaire:* Rejoice), rendered by the Latin "Ave" or the English "Hail." Compare Catullus' greeting: "Ave atque vale" (hail and farewell). In everyday Greek usage the word means "hello" or "good-bye."

lost day's dawn: In Greek, αὐγὴ χαμένης μέρας (*auge chamenes meras*), a deliberate misquotation of a verse from the *Salutations* (oikos 5): Χαῖρε αὐγὴ μυστικῆς ἡμέρας (*Chaire auge mystikes hemeras:* Hail the mystical day's dawn).

Zero Star Brandy

Nauplion (or Nafplio) is a small port in the Peloponnese that became the first capital of Greece in 1829; Euboea and Skopelos are Greek islands.

The Rare Gift

Come and get them: In Greek, μολὼν λαβέ (*molôn labé*). According to Plutarch, these are the words Leonidas, king of Sparta, addressed to the Persians who asked him to surrender at the Battle of Thermopylae.

Lower Class

This is the third poem of a trilogy inspired by a visit to Olympia. A roman numeral appears below each title.

The Temple of Hera (Heraion), the Nymphaeum or Exedra of Herodes Atticus, and the Prytaneion are situated in the ancient sanctuary of Olympia in Elis.

Saint Constantine and Saint Helen's Day

During his reign as Emperor of Rome (306–337), Constantine the Great — also known as Constantine I, or Saint Constantine (c. 272–337) — transformed the ancient Greek colony of Byzantium into the imperial capital of the Roman Empire. As Constantinople it would remain the capital of the Eastern Roman Empire for more than a millennium. He was the first Roman emperor to convert to Christianity. The Orthodox Church keeps his feast on May 21, along with that of his mother, Empress Saint Helen.

Among the Greek Orthodox it is customary to visit the graves of deceased family members or friends on their respective name days, as well as to bring a list of the names of the deceased to one's priest for commemoration, prayer, and blessing. On this occasion, a holy bread, the *prosforon*, is offered; its name derives from προσφορά (*prosfora*: offering). It bears a round seal marked with the symbols of Jesus Christ, the Virgin Mary, the angels, and the saints.

Athanasios (Athos) Dimoulas (1921–1985), a civil engineer and award-winning poet, was Kiki Dimoula's husband.

Incident

Slaughtered, while Golden: an allusion to two events in the myth of Medea and Jason. Medea helped Jason steal the Golden Fleece. She later murdered their children after Jason repudiated her in order to marry the daughter of Creon, the king of Corinth.

Mother of the Floor Below

The antepenultimate line of this poem's version differs slightly from that published by Ikaros because Kiki Dimoula authorized us to replace the adjective μαύρη (black) with κόκκινη (red).

Saint Lazarus' Day

In Greek Orthodox tradition, Saint Lazarus' Day is the Saturday preceding Holy Week. According to the Gospel of John, Jesus performed the miracle of restoring Lazarus of Bethany to life four days after his death (John 11:14–44).

The ancient Greek adjective μωραί, feminine plural of μωρός (*moros: foolish*), makes reference to the Parable of the Wise and the Foolish Virgins (Matthew 25:1–13).

An allusion is made to another miracle performed by Jesus, the healing of the lame man at the pool in Bethesda (John 5:8): "Jesus saith unto him, Rise, take up thy bed, and walk."

Transportation of Remains—Theophany

Because burial space is scarce in Greece, the dead may be buried in a temporary grave for a period of one to five years, after which the remains are exhumed, washed with wine, perfumed, and placed in a small ossuary of wood or metal kept in a special room of the cemetery.

Theophany (Θεοφάνεια: *Theophaneia*), or Epiphany (God's Revelation), celebrated on January 6, commemorates the baptism of Jesus in the Jordan River and the apparition of the Holy Trinity.

Diabolical Coincidence

This version of the poem differs slightly from the one first published because Kiki Dimoula subsequently advised us to remove the poem's last line.

WORKS BY KIKI DIMOULA

Publications in Greek

Ἔρεβος [Erebus]. Athens: Privately published, 1956; 2nd ed. Athens: Stigmi, 1990.

Ἐρήμην [In Absentia]. Athens: Difros, 1958; 2nd ed., Athens: Stigmi, 1990.

Ἐπὶ τὰ ἴχνη [On the Track]. Athens: Fexis, 1963; 2nd ed., Athens: Stigmi, 1989.

Τὸ Λίγο τοῦ κόσμου [The Little of the World]. Athens: Privately published, 1971; 2nd ed., Athens: Nefeli, 1983; 3rd ed., Athens: Stigmi, 1990.

Τὸ τελευταῖο σῶμα μου [My Last Body]. Athens: Keimena, 1981; 2nd ed., Athens: Stigmi, 1989.

Χαῖρε ποτὲ [Hail Never]. Athens: Stigmi, 1988.

Ἡ ἐφηβεία τῆς λήθης [Oblivion's Adolescence]. Athens: Stigmi, 1994.

Ποιήματα [Poems]. Athens: Ikaros, 1998.

Ἑνὸς λεπτοῦ μαζὶ [A Moment of Two]. Athens: Ikaros, 1998.

Ἦχος ἀπομακρύνσεων [Sound of Distancings]. Athens: Ikaros, 2001.

Ὁ φιλοπαίγμων μῦθος [The Frolicsome Fable]. Speech, Greek Academy, November 11, 2003. Athens: Ikaros, 2003.

Ἐκτός σχεδίου [Unplanned]. Selections from the Bank of Greece magazine Ὁ Κύκλος [Ho Kyklos]. Athens: Ikaros, 2004.

Χλόη θερμοκηπίου [Greenhouse Grass]. Athens: Ikaros, 2005.

Μεταφερθήκαμε παραπλεύρως [We've Moved Next Door]. Athens: Ikaros, 2007.

Ἔρανος σκέψεων γιὰ τὴν ἀνέγερση τίτλου ὑπὲρ τῆς ἀστέγου αὐτῆς ὁμιλίας [Thoughtraising . . .]. Speech, Archaeological Society, Athens, January 26, 2009. Athens: Ikaros, 2009.

Τὰ εὕρετρα [The Finder's Reward]. Athens: Ikaros, 2010.

Selected Translations

Albanian

Dhimula, Kiki. *Pasqyra e mbrëmjes: poezi.* Trans. Niko Kacalidha. Tiranë: Toena, 2010.

Danish

Dimoula, Kiki. *Glemselens pubertet: udvalgte digte.* Trans. Vibeke Espholm. Århus: Husets Forlag, 2002.

English

Dimoula, Kiki. *Lethe's Adolescence.* Trans. David Connolly. Minneapolis: Nostos, 1996.

———. *What Sea? 20 Poems.* Trans. Olga Broumas. *The Drunken Boat* 9, nos. 1–11 (2011), available at http://www.thedrunkenboat.com/kikidimoula.html.

French

Dimoula, Kiki. *Du peu du monde et autres poèmes.* Trans. Martine Plateau-Zygounas. Paris: La Différence, 1995 [bilingual].

———. *Mon dernier corps.* Trans. Michel Volkovitch. Paris: Cahiers grecs, 1995; bilingual edition: Paris-Orbey: Arfuyen, 2010.

———. *Je te salue jamais.* Trans. Michel Volkovitch. Paris: Desmos / Cahiers grecs, 1997 [bilingual].

———. *Anthologie de Kiki Dimoula.* Trans. Eurydice Trichon-Milsani. Paris: L'Harmattan, 2007.

———. « *Le peu du monde* » suivi de « *Je te salue jamais* ». Trans. Michel Volkovitch. Preface by Nikos Dimou. Paris: Gallimard, 2010.

German

Dimoula, Kiki. *Eine Minute zusammen / Gedichte.* Trans. Evangelia Karamountzou. Frankfurt am Main: Dielmann, 2000.

———. *Gedichte: 1959 bis 2000.* Trans. Evangelia Karamountzou, Georgi Fotopoulos, and Niki Lambrianidou. Frankfurt am Main: Dielmann, 2001.

————. *Plötzlich wurde ich hellhörig: Gedichte und Der spielerische Mythos*, Trans. Dadi Sideri-Speck. Cologne: Romiosini, 2008.

————. *Erlebt*. Trans. Dadi Sideri-Speck. Ills. Jannis Psychopedis. Cologne: Romiosini, 2010 [bilingual].

Italian

Dimulà, Kikí. *L'adolescenza dell'oblio*. Trans. Paola Maria Minucci. Milan: Crocetti, 2000 [bilingual].

Serbian

Димула, Кики [Dimula, Kiki]. *Песме* [Pesme]. Trans. Гага Росић [Gaga Rosic]. Београд [Belgrade]: Артист [Artist], 2002.

Spanish

Dimoula, Kiki. *Poemas*. Trans. Nina Anghelidis-Spinedi. Buenos Aires: El Imaginero, 1989.

————. *31 poemas*. Trans. Nina Anghelidis and Carlos Spinedi. Buenos Aires: Nuevohacer, 1998.

Dimulá, Kikí. *Símbolos solubles*. Trans. Nina Anghelidis. Ourense: Linteo, 2010.

Swedish

Dimoula, Kiki. *Från mina rum: Dikter i urval*. Trans. Håkan Edgren. Ills. Claes Tellvid. Lund: Ellerströms, 1997.

————. *Glömskans pubertet*. Trans. Ingemar Rhedin. Solna: Axion, 1997 [bilingual].

————. *Var hälsad aldrig*. Trans. Ingemar Rhedin. Solna: Axion, 2002; 2nd ed., 2004 [bilingual].

————. *På spåren*. Trans. Ingemar Rhedin. Solna: Axion, 2004 [bilingual].

Poems Collected in English Anthologies

Poems by Kiki Dimoula are also included in various Bulgarian, Finnish, French, German, Italian, Polish, and Spanish anthologies.

City Lights Anthology. Trans. Eleni Fourtouni and Bertrand Mathieu. San Francisco: City Light Books, 1975.

Contemporary Greek Women Poets. Trans. Eleni Fourtouni. New Haven, Conn.: Thelphini Press, 1978.

Contemporary Greek Poetry. Trans. Kimon Friar. Athens: Greek Ministry of Culture, 1985.

Daughters of Sappho: Contemporary Greek Women Poets. Trans. Rae Dalven. Rutherford, N.J.: Fairleigh Dickinson University Press, 1994.

Grind the Big Tooth: A Collection of Contemporary Greek Poetry. Trans. Robert Crist. Pittsburgh: Sterling House, 1998.

Greek Writers Today: An Anthology. Ed. David Connolly. Dimoula's poems trans. David Connolly. Athens: Hellenic Authors' Society, 2003.

Modern Greek Poetry: An Anthology. Ed. Nanos Valaoritis and Thanasis Maskaleris. Jersey City, N.J.: Talisman House, 2003.

A Century of Greek Poetry, 1900–2000. Ed. Peter Bien, Peter Constantine, Edmund Keeley, and Karen Van Dyck. Dimoula's poems trans. Karen Van Dyck, Katerina Anghelaki-Rooke, Philip Ramp, Don Schofield, Harita Mona, and David Connolly. Hillsdale, N.J.: Cosmos, 2004.

The Greek Poets: Homer to the Present. Ed. Peter Constantine, Rachel Hadas, Edmund Keeley, Karen Van Dyck. Dimoula's poems trans. Olga Broumas. New York: Norton, 2010.

ACKNOWLEDGMENTS

The translators gratefully acknowledge the editors of the following periodicals in which these English poems first appeared, some in slightly different form.

Boston Review (July–August 2012) for "Essential Difference."
James Dickey Review 28, no. 1 (Fall 2011), for "Melancholy" and "Diabolical Coincidence."
Literary Imagination 14, no. 2 (July 2012), for "I Do Not Know" and "Repair Loans."
Notre Dame Review 34 (July 2012) for "It Will Come Out to Scold You."

Cecile Inglessis Margellos's Acknowledgments

My sincerest thanks to John Donatich of Yale University Press for perceptively intuiting Kiki Dimoula's poetic genius through my first stammering samples of translation, for encouraging me to pursue it, and for letting me miss every possible deadline; to Senior Editor Jennifer Banks for her propitious idea of a collaboration between Rika Lesser and me, and for her unremitting, tactful support; to Senior Manuscript Editor Susan Laity for her impressively proficient editing, and for her talent in walking a tightrope between two equally compulsive translators.

On this side of the Atlantic, I would like to warmly thank Katerina Karydi and Marilena Panourgia of Ikaros for unhesitatingly trusting me with their precious poet; Mary and Alexis Caniaris for offering the mesmerizing art of the late Vlassis Caniaris for the dust jacket of our book; Mary Kitroef for her valuable help in the translation and pre-editing of this book's front matter, and for her smiling voice; the novelist Stratis Haviaras and the poet Nasos Vagenas for their constructive critique and substantial advice; my family for their stimulating confidence, and for not scolding me when I took up smoking again; and my friends for stoically enduring my absences and absentmindedness.

My greatest debt of gratitude is, however, owed to Kiki Dimoula for her unwavering faith in me: it gave me wings to fly toward her stellar poetry through translation.

Rika Lesser's Acknowledgments

Heartfelt thanks to my two dearest friends in the arts of poetry and translation, Rosanna Warren and Richard Howard. They provided moral support wherever I wandered in the woods of the unknown language, as did my sister, Joan Japha. I particularly want to thank Richard for patiently enduring successive drafts of poems I could not fully explain, and for lending me the comfort of his insight and wisdom.

I commend Ingemar Rhedin for his work in Swedish on Kiki Dimoula, and I would like to express my gratitude to Jonas Ellerström, Jan Henrik Swahn, and Magnus William-Olsson for putting Swedish translations of the poet they published, translated, or owned, respectively, into my hands.

AUTHOR INFORMATION

Kiki Dimoula

Kiki Dimoula, the most celebrated contemporary Greek poet, was born in Athens in 1931. From 1949 to 1974 she worked as a clerk for the Bank of Greece. She was married to the civil engineer and poet Athos Dimoulas (1921–1985), and is the mother of two.

In 1956 she published her first volume of poetry, *Erebus*. Eleven more volumes of poetry and three volumes of prose have appeared to date. Since 1998, her books have been published by Ikaros, the prestigious publisher of the two Greek Nobel laureates, George Seferis and Odysseas Elytis.

Dimoula has been awarded Greece's most distinguished national prizes: the Second National Prize (for *The Little of the World*, 1972) and First National Prize (for *Hail Never*, 1989), the Ouranis Prize of the Academy of Athens (for *Oblivion's Adolescence*, 1995), the Aristeion of Letters of the Academy of Athens (2001), and the Grand National Prize for lifetime achievement (2010). In 2009 she was awarded the European Literature Prize by the Association Capitale Européenne des Littératures.

In 2002 she became the third woman elected a full member of the Academy of Athens.

Cecile Inglessis Margellos

Born in 1953 in Athens, Cecile Inglessis Margellos moved to Paris with her family in 1969 and to Geneva with her husband, businessman Theodore Margellos, in 1980. She now divides her time between Geneva and Athens.

Margellos holds a diploma from the Institute of Political Sciences of Paris (Sciences-Po, 1975), a license in sociology (Paris X, 1975), and a Diplôme d'Études Supérieures French literature (University of Geneva, 1997). She has worked for the Permanent Greek Delegations to the Organisation for Economic Co-operation and Development (OECD) in Paris and to the United Nations in Geneva.

Margellos is a scholar specializing in sixteenth-century French literature, a literary translator, and a critic. She has translated fiction, essays, and poetry, including works by Antoine Berman, Colette, Pierre Drieu La Rochelle, Jean Giraudoux, Molière, and Raymond Queneau and three works by Louis-Férdinand Céline: *Journey to the End of the Night* (2007), *Conversations with Professor Y* (2010), and *Death on Credit* (forthcoming, 2013). Her annotated translation of Plato's *Symposium* from ancient to modern Greek will be published in 2013. She is a contributing writer and reviewer for the Greek newspaper *Vima* as well as for a number of literary magazines.

She has been married to Theodore Margellos since 1979, and they have a daughter, Iliodora, an artist. Theodore and Cecile Inglessis Margellos founded the Margellos World Republic of Letters in 2007.

Rika Lesser

Born in Brooklyn, New York, in 1953, Rika Lesser took an early interest in the sciences but graduated from Yale with a B.A. summa cum laude in 1974. She holds an M.F.A. from Columbia University School of the Arts (Writing, 1977). She is the author of four collections of poetry, *Etruscan Things* (Braziller, 1983; rev. ed. Sheep Meadow Press, 2010), *All We Need of Hell* (University of North Texas Press, 1995), *Growing Back* (University of South Carolina Press, 1997), and *Questions of Love: New and Selected Poems* (Sheep Meadow Press, 2008). She has translated and published collections of poetry by Göran Sonnevi, Gunnar Ekelöf, and Claes Andersson, as well as Rainer Maria Rilke and Hermann Hesse (including *Siddhartha: An Indic Poem*, Barnes & Noble Classics, 2007). She also translates books for children and readers of all ages from Swedish and German.

Lesser has been the recipient of the Amy Lowell Travelling Poetry Scholarship (1974–75), an Ingram-Merrill Foundation Award for Poetry Writing (1978–79), fellowships from the Fulbright Foundation (1999) and the National Endowment for the Arts (2001, 2013), the Harold Morton Landon Translation Prize from the Academy of American Poets (1982), two Poetry Translation Prizes of the Swedish Academy (1996, 2010), and other awards. The American-Scandinavian Foundation gave her its Translation Prize twice—in 1992 for selections from Sonnevi's *A Child Is Not a Knife*, and in 2002 for selections from *Mozart's Third Brain*, subsequently shortlisted for the 2010 PEN Award for Poetry in Translation. A teacher of poetry and literary translation, an authorized student teacher of *Feldenkrais Awareness Through Movement* lessons, she makes her home in Brooklyn Heights.